NATIONAL GEOGRAPHIC LEARNING | CENGAGE Learning

3

READING
EXPLORER

NANCY DOUGLAS • DAVID BOHLKE

Second Edition

NATIONAL GEOGRAPHIC LEARNING | CENGAGE Learning

Australia • Brazil • Japan • Korea • Mexico • Singapore • Spain • United Kingdom • United States

D0074580

Reading Explorer 3, Second Edition
Nancy Douglas and David Bohlke

Publisher: Andrew Robinson

Executive Editor: Sean Bermingham

Senior Development Editor: Derek Mackrell

Associate Development Editors:
 Ridhima Thakral, Michelle Harris

Assistant Editor: Melissa Pang

Director of Global Marketing: Ian Martin

Product Marketing Manager: Lindsey Miller

Senior Director of Production:
 Michael Burggren

Senior Content Project Manager: Tan Jin Hock

Manufacturing Planner: Mary Beth Hennebury

Compositor: Page 2, LLC.

Cover/Text Design: Creative Director:
 Christopher Roy, Art Director: Scott Baker,
 Designer: Alex Dull

Cover Photo: Jonathan Andrew/Corbis

Student Book with Online Workbook:
ISBN-13: 978-1-305-25448-0

Student Book:
ISBN-13: 978-1-285-84691-0

National Geographic Learning
20 Channel Center Street
Boston, MA 02210
USA

Cengage Learning is a leading provider of customized learning solutions with office locations around the globe, including Singapore, the United Kingdom, Australia, Mexico, Brazil, and Japan.

Cengage Learning products are represented in Canada by Nelson Education, Ltd.

Visit National Geographic Learning online at **ngl.cengage.com**

Visit our corporate website at **www.cengage.com**

Printed in the United States of America
7 8 9 10 11 12   23 22 21 20 19 18

Contents

Scope and Sequence

Welcome to Reading Explorer!

In this book, you'll travel the globe, explore different cultures, and discover new ways of looking at the world. You'll also become a better reader!

What's new in the Second Edition?

New and updated topics

Explore the power of our planet, the nature of risk, and our future life in space.

New Reading Skill section

Learn how to read strategically—and think critically as you read.

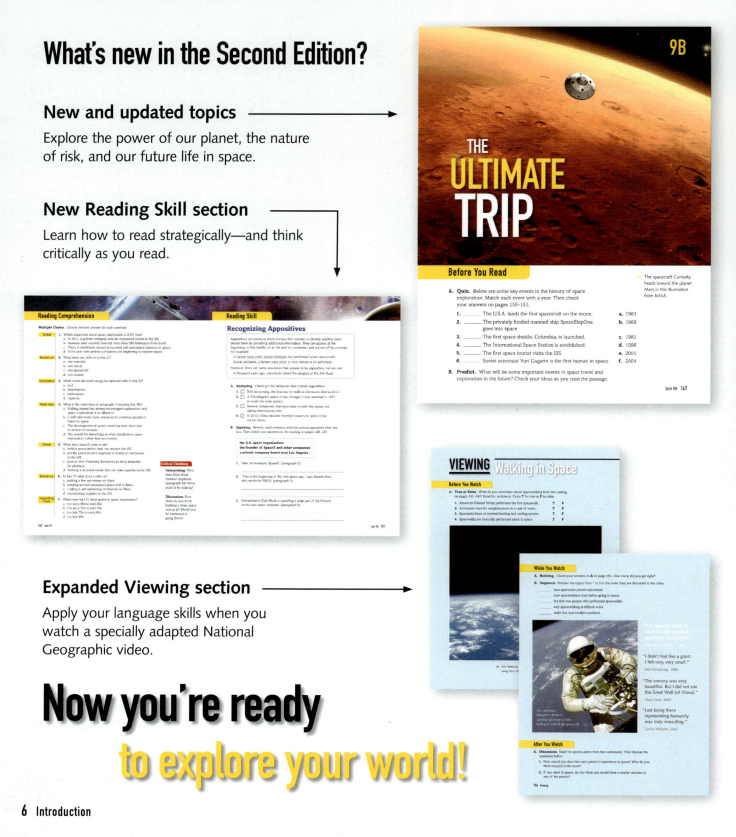

> The spacecraft Curiosity heads toward the planet Mars in this illustration from NASA.

Expanded Viewing section

Apply your language skills when you watch a specially adapted National Geographic video.

Now you're ready
to explore your world!

SPORT AND FITNESS

Hurdlers racing in
Guangzhou, China

Warm Up

Discuss these questions with a partner.

1. What sports are popular in your country?

2. Are any sports from your country popular in other countries?

3. Which types of athletes do you think are the fittest?

A WORLD OF SOCCER

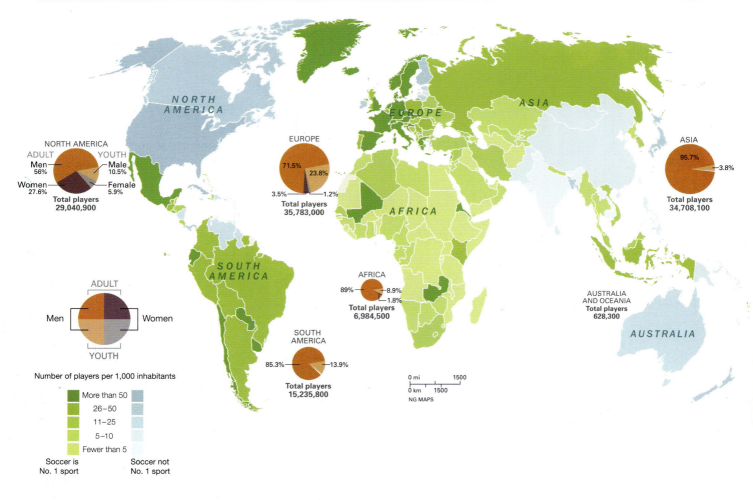

NORTH AMERICA
ADULT — YOUTH
Men 56% — Male 10.5%
Women 27.6% — Female 5.9%
Total players 29,040,900

EUROPE
71.5% — 23.8%
3.5% — 1.2%
Total players 35,783,000

ASIA
95.7% — 3.8%
Total players 34,708,100

AFRICA
89% — 8.9% — 1.8%
Total players 6,984,500

SOUTH AMERICA
85.3% — 13.9%
Total players 15,235,800

AUSTRALIA AND OCEANIA
Total players 628,300

ADULT
Men — Women
YOUTH

Number of players per 1,000 inhabitants

- More than 50
- 26–50
- 11–25
- 5–10
- Fewer than 5

Soccer is No. 1 sport   Soccer not No. 1 sport

0 mi 1500
0 km 1500
NG MAPS

Before You Read

A. True or False. Look at the information above. Read the sentences below and circle **T** (True) or **F** (False).

1. Soccer is the most popular sport in most countries of the world.   **T**   **F**

2. The continent with the largest number of soccer players is Asia.   **T**   **F**

3. More women play soccer in South America than in North America.   **T**   **F**

4. In most countries in western Europe, there are more than 50 players per 1,000 inhabitants.   **T**   **F**

B. Predict. Why is soccer such a popular sport? Make a list of your ideas. Then read the passage. Underline all the reasons that are mentioned. How many of your ideas are discussed?

THE WORLD'S GAME

A dirt soccer field in Agahozo Shalom Youth Village, Rwanda

1 Throughout history, humans have played some kind of kicking game.

What the world now calls football, or soccer in the U.S., began as far back as 2500 B.C.E. with the Chinese game of *tsu chu*. The sport we know today originated in Britain. By the 1840s, England's Football Association **established** a set of rules, and the modern game was born. Today, more than 120 million players all over the globe **participate** in the game, truly making soccer the world's sport.

So, why is soccer so popular? Maybe it's the game's camaraderie:[1] the feeling that the team on the field is *your* team; their win is *your* **victory**, and their loss is *your* **defeat**. Or maybe it's the game's international quality. In countries like France, England, Spain, and Brazil, major teams have players from many different nations, and these clubs now have fans all over the world. Or perhaps it's the promise of great wealth. A number of professional soccer players, including Cameroon's Samuel Eto'o and Portugal's Cristiano Ronaldo, come from poor families. Today, both of these players make millions of euros every year.

Soccer is popular for all of these reasons, but ultimately, the main reason for its **universal** appeal may be this: It's a simple game. It can be played anywhere with anything—a ball, a can, or even some bags tied together. And anyone can play it. "You don't need to be rich . . . to play soccer," says historian Peter Alegi. "You just need a flat space and a ball."

---

1 **Camaraderie** is a feeling of friendship or team spirit among people who share an experience together.

Children in the Democratic Republic of the Congo play soccer with a ball made of string and tape.

35　It is this **unique** simplicity that makes soccer the most popular sport in Africa. Here, even in rural areas far from the bright lights and big stadiums, children and adults play the game, often with handmade balls.

40 ## A Passion[2] for Soccer

The story of soccer in Africa is a long one. In the mid-1800s, European colonists[3] brought the game to Africa. Early matches were first played in the South African cities of Cape
45　Town and Port Elizabeth in 1862, and in time, the sport spread across the continent. In the past century, as countries in Africa urbanized and became independent, they joined the International Federation of Association Football
50　(FIFA). Today, some of the game's best players come from African nations, including Cameroon, Ivory Coast, Ghana, and Nigeria, and all over the continent, thousands of soccer academies now recruit boys from poorer cities and towns to
55　play the game. Many learn to play in their bare feet,[4] and they are tough, creative **competitors**. Their dream is to join a national team or one of the big clubs in Europe someday. For some, the dream comes true, but for most, it doesn't.

---

2 Passion is a powerful emotion or feeling.

3 Colonists are people from one country who take control of another country.

4 If you do something **in your bare feet**, you do it without shoes.

In Johannesburg, South Africa, a group of fans cheer on their team.

60 But joining a professional team and making a lot of money isn't the main reason that soccer is so popular all over Africa, says Abubakari Abdul-Ganiyu, a teacher who works with youth clubs in Tamale, Ghana. "Soccer is
65 the passion of everyone here," he says. "It **unifies** us." In fact, more than once, the game has helped to bring people together. In Ivory Coast, for example, immigrants[5] and Muslims faced discrimination[6] for years. Yet
70 many of the country's best soccer players are from Muslim and immigrant families. As a result, the national team has become a symbol of unity and has helped to **promote** peace throughout the country.

75 All over Africa, soccer is popular with parents and teachers for another reason: It keeps young people—especially boys—in school and out of trouble. "Most clubs in Tamale, Ghana, don't allow boys to play if they don't go to
80 school," explains Abubakari. "We're trying our best to help young people and to make them **responsible** in society. Soccer helps us do this. For us, soccer is also a tool for hope."

---

5 An **immigrant** is a person who comes to live in a country from another country.

6 If you **face discrimination**, you are not treated fairly by others in society.

Reading Comprehension

Multiple Choice. Choose the best answer for each question.

Gist 1. What is this passage mainly about?
- a. the history of soccer
- b. soccer clubs
- c. the popularity of soccer
- d. how African soccer began

Detail 2. In the second paragraph, which of these is NOT given as a possible reason for soccer's popularity?
- a. the team spirit among players
- b. famous players from many different countries
- c. the number of soccer games shown on TV
- d. the possibility of making a lot of money

Detail 3. What does the author mean by *It's a simple game.* (line 29)
- a. The rules are easy for people to understand.
- b. You can play it anywhere with anything.
- c. You don't need talent to play soccer well.
- d. There are many local versions of soccer.

Detail 4. Where did soccer originate in Africa?
- a. Ivory Coast
- b. Ghana
- c. South Africa
- d. Cameroon

Reference 5. What does *some* refer to in line 58?
- a. poor boys
- b. soccer academies
- c. national teams
- d. cities and towns

Detail 6. Which of these statements about the Ivory Coast national team is NOT true?
- a. Many of its best players are from immigrant families.
- b. There are Muslim players on the team.
- c. One of its players is Abubakari Abdul-Ganiyu.
- d. It has helped to encourage peace in the country.

Main Idea 7. What is the main idea of the last paragraph?
- a. More schools in Africa are opening soccer clubs.
- b. Soccer helps people get better grades in school.
- c. Soccer helps young people be more responsible.
- d. Older soccer players help younger ones fit into society.

Critical Thinking

Evaluating: The writer states that soccer can help *bring people together.* What evidence is given to support the claim? In what ways might a sport such as soccer divide people rather than bring them together?

_____

Discussion: Do you agree with the writer's arguments for why soccer is so popular? What other reasons could account for its global popularity?

Scanning for Specific Information

Scanning is reading a text quickly to find specific pieces of information. Try these tips to help you scan effectively.

1. Decide what kind of information you need to scan for—a number, a person's name, a specific word or phrase, etc. Keep that word or phrase in mind as you read. For example, if you are scanning for the names of people or places, look for capitalized words.

2. Analyze the text before you scan. If the text is long, you may want to skim it first to determine where the information is likely to be.

3. Run your eyes over several lines of text at a time. When you find what you are searching for, read the entire sentence.

A. Scanning. For each item (1–5), decide what kind of information you need to scan for (for example, a place or a time). Then scan the reading on page 9, and note the answers.

1. when soccer first began _____

2. where soccer first began _____

3. where modern soccer began _____

4. when modern soccer began _____

5. a famous player from Portugal _____

B. Scanning. Scan the reading on pages 9–11 and circle **T** (True) or **F** (False) for each of the sentences below.

1. Cristiano Ronaldo is from a rich family.   **T   F**

2. Soccer is popular in Africa because of its simplicity.   **T   F**

3. Soccer spread in Africa from south to north.   **T   F**

4. Many of Ivory Coast's best players are from Muslim and immigrant families.   **T   F**

5. Abubakari Abdul-Ganiyu describes soccer as a tool for hope.   **T   F**

Vocabulary Practice

A. Completion. Complete the information by circling the correct word in each pair.

Over the past two decades, Asian soccer-playing nations such as Japan, China, and South Korea have worked together to raise interest in the sport. This led to the first World Cup to be held in Asia, in 2002. The **1. (competition / defeat)** was **2. (unique / universal)** because it was co-hosted by two countries: South Korea and Japan. A total of 32 teams **3. (participated / established)** in the tournament. The eventual winner was Brazil, who achieved **4. (defeat / victory)** by beating Germany 2–0 in the final. Overall, the event was a great success: It helped to **5. (participate / promote)** cooperation among nations and was **6. (responsible / unified)** for creating a new generation of soccer fans across Asia.

⌄ Brazil's Ronaldo holds up the trophy after beating Germany in the World Cup final in Yokohama, Japan, in 2002.

B. Words in Context. Complete each sentence with the correct answer.

1. If someone **establishes** something (e.g., an organization), they _____ it.
   a. create   b. destroy

2. In sports, if you **defeat** another team, you _____.
   a. win and they lose   b. lose and they win

3. If something is **universal**, it relates to _____ in the world.
   a. few people   b. all people

4. Something or someone that **unifies** people causes them to _____.
   a. come together   b. separate

> **Word Link** The prefix **uni-** means "one" or "single," e.g., *unify, universal, unique, unite, uniform.*

WHAT MAKES AN ⬭⬭⬭ OLYMPIC CHAMPION?

Before You Read

A. Completion. Read the information below and complete sentences 1–4 using the correct form of the words in **bold**.

Several **athletes** made headlines during the 2012 London **Olympics**. Some, like Usain Bolt, broke Olympic records after many years of **training**. Considered the fastest runner ever, "Lightning" Bolt continued his winning streak when he won gold **medals** in the 100-meter and 200-meter races.

1. Usain Bolt is one of the world's most famous _____.

2. _____ is an essential part of preparing for a sports competition.

3. The world's biggest athletics competition is the _____.

4. When people achieve something special, they are awarded _____.

B. Discussion. Discuss these questions. Then read the passage to learn more about Olympic athletes.

1. Do you think anyone can train to become an Olympic athlete?

2. Do you think the life of an Olympic athlete is enjoyable? Why or why not?

∧ Usain Bolt crosses the finish line to win the 100-meter gold medal in the 2012 London Olympics.

A girl swims during a training session at Hangzhou Chen Jinglun Sport School Natatorium, where Chinese Olympic swimmer Ye Shiwen also trained.

1　How does a person become an Olympic champion—someone capable of winning the gold? In reality, a combination of biological,

5　environmental, and psychological factors, as well as training and practice, all go into making a super athlete.

　　Perhaps the most important factor involved in

10　becoming an elite[1] athlete is genetics. Most Olympic competitors are equipped with certain physical characteristics that differentiate them from the average person. Take an elite athlete's muscles, for example. In most human skeletal

15　muscles (the ones that make your body move), there are fast-twitch fibers[2] and slow-twitch fibers. Fast-twitch fibers help us move quickly. Olympic weightlifters, for example, have a large number of fast-twitch fibers in their

20　muscles—many more than the average person. These allow them to lift hundreds of kilos from the ground and over their heads in seconds. Surprisingly, a large, muscular body is not the main requirement to do well in this sport. It

25　is more important to have a large number of fast-twitch fibers in the muscles.

1　**Elite** refers to the most powerful, rich, or talented people within a particular group.

2　Muscle **fibers** are thin, threadlike pieces of flesh that make up the muscles in your body.

> ## "You have less than three seconds from takeoff until you hit the water, so it has to be reflex."
> Greg Louganis

The legs of an elite marathon runner, on the other hand, might contain up to 90 percent slow-twitch muscle fibers. These **generate** energy efficiently and enable an athlete to control fatigue and keep moving for a longer period of time. When we exercise long or hard, it's common to experience tiredness, muscle pain, and difficulty breathing. These feelings are caused when the muscles produce high amounts of lactate[3] and can't remove it quickly enough. Athletes with many slow-twitch muscle fibers seem to be able to clear the lactate from their muscles faster as they move. Thus, the average runner might start to feel discomfort halfway into a race. A trained Olympic athlete, however, might not feel pain until much later in the competition.

For some Olympic competitors, size is important. Most male champion swimmers are 180 cm (six feet) or taller, allowing them to reach longer and swim faster. For both male and female gymnasts, though, a smaller size and body weight mean they can move with greater ease, and are less likely to suffer damage when landing on the floor from a height of up to 4.5 meters (15 feet).

Some athletes' abilities are naturally **enhanced** by their environment. Those raised at high altitudes in countries such as Kenya, Ethiopia, and Morocco have blood that is rich in hemoglobin. Large amounts of hemoglobin carry oxygen[4] around the body faster, enabling these athletes to run better. Cultural factors also help some athletes do well at certain sports. Tegla Loroupe, a young woman from northern Kenya, has won several marathons. She **attributes** some of her success to her country's altitude (she trains at about 2,400 meters, or 8,000 feet) and some to her cultural background. As a child, she had to run ten kilometers to school every day. "I'd be punished if I was late," she says.

Although genetics, environment, and even culture play a part in becoming an elite athlete, training and practice are needed to succeed. Marathon runners may be able to control fatigue and keep moving for long periods of time, but they must train to reach and maintain their goals. Weightlifters and gymnasts perfect their skills by repeating the same **motions** again and again until they are **automatic**. Greg Louganis, winner of four Olympic diving gold medals, says divers must train the same way to be successful: "You have less than three seconds from takeoff until you hit the water, so it has to be reflex. You have to repeat the dives hundreds, maybe thousands, of times." Training this way requires an athlete to be not only physically fit but psychologically healthy as well. "They have to be," says Sean McCann, a sports psychologist at the Olympic Training Center in the U.S. "Otherwise, they couldn't handle the training loads we put on them. [Athletes] have to be good at setting goals, generating energy when they need it, and managing anxiety."

How do athletes **adjust** to such intense pressure? Louganis explains how he learned to control his anxiety during a competition: "Most divers think too much . . . ," he says. "They're too much in their heads. What worked for me was humor. I remember thinking about what my mother would say if she saw me do a bad dive. She'd probably just compliment[5] me on the beautiful splash."[6]

---

3 **Lactate** is a substance produced by your muscles when you have been exercising a lot.

4 **Oxygen** is a colorless gas in the air that is needed by all plants and animals.

5 If you **compliment** someone, you say something polite about their appearance or something they did.

6 A **splash** is the sound made when something hits water or falls into it.

Reading Comprehension

Multiple Choice. Choose the best answer for each question.

Gist

1. What is this reading mainly about?
   a. factors that make someone a super athlete
   b. the different muscle types of a super athlete
   c. the size of a super athlete
   d. how to qualify for the Olympics

Reference

2. The word *more* in line 20 refers to ___.
   a. Olympic weightlifters
   b. fast-twitch fibers
   c. muscles
   d. average people

Inference

3. Having a lot of slow-twitch muscle fibers is particularly important for ___.
   a. cyclists
   b. divers
   c. weightlifters
   d. table tennis players

Detail

4. When lactate builds up in their muscles, people feel ___.
   a. strength
   b. energy
   c. dizziness
   d. pain

Detail

5. What advantage do athletes from high-altitude countries have?
   a. a strong sense of culture
   b. hemoglobin-rich blood
   c. lower amounts of lactate in their muscles
   d. more muscles in their legs

Main Idea

6. What is the main idea of the sixth paragraph (starting line 69)?
   a. Genetics is an important part of athletic success.
   b. Divers must train to be successful.
   c. Marathon runners must train hard to succeed.
   d. Success in sports comes from a lot of practice.

Inference

7. What statement would diver Greg Louganis probably agree with?
   a. Athletes cannot perform well unless they are under pressure.
   b. It's key to practice and train hard, but try not to take things too seriously.
   c. It's important to joke around with your teammates before you perform any sport.
   d. A professional athlete should never feel anxiety.

Critical Thinking

Interpreting: What do you think Louganis means when he says most divers are *too much in their heads*? How might this affect an athlete's performance?

_____

Discussion: One of the aims of the Olympic Games is to improve relationships among countries. Do you think they achieve this?

Classifying Information

When you classify information, you organize it. There are several ways to classify information. For example, you can classify sports and activities by those that emphasize speed vs. those that emphasize strength. Or you could classify sports by those that are more popular with men vs. those more popular with women. T-charts (**A** below) and Venn diagrams (**B** below) are two ways to classify information.

A. Classification. Write **a–h** in the chart to classify each of the following sports in three different ways.

a. baseball	**b.** boxing	**c.** bowling	**d.** golf
e. soccer	**f.** surfing	**g.** table tennis	**h.** weightlifting

Sports that use a ball	Sports that don't use a ball

Sports usually played in teams	Sports usually not played in teams

Sports that you think are exciting to watch	Sports that you think are not exciting to watch

B. Classification. According to the reading, are the following important to marathon runners, to gymnasts, or to both? Write each answer (**a–f**) in the correct place in the chart.

a. training
b. slow-twitch muscles
c. repeated motions
d. psychological health
e. small body size
f. ability to control fatigue and keep moving for a long time

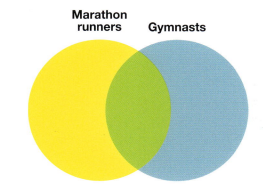

Marathon runners   Gymnasts

Vocabulary Practice

A. Completion. Complete the information with the correct form of words from the box. Three words are extra.

adjust	**attribute**	**automatic**
champion	**differentiate**	**enhance**
generate	**genetic**	**motion**
psychological		

In September 2013, **1.** _____ swimmer Diana Nyad became the first person to swim from Cuba to the U.S. state of Florida without using a shark cage. She had unsuccessfully attempted the 177-kilometer (110-mile) swim several times before, but at age 64, she finally completed the historic swim. In total, she spent a little under 53 hours in constant **2.** _____ in the water. She was fit, had a team along to help her, and wore a special suit and mask to keep jellyfish off her skin. Some suggested this equipment **3.** _____ her swimming speed, though Nyad claimed it actually slowed her down.

What **4.** _____ this successful attempt from Nyad's four previous attempts? Experts **5.** _____ her success to Nyad's mental determination. They believe that her struggle was just as much **6.** _____ as physical. She was not allowed to grab the boat when the water was rough, because this would **7.** _____ disqualify her. Her determination was so strong that even though she felt sick for much of the journey, she never gave up.

∧ U.S. swimmer Diana Nyad swam across the treacherous Florida Straits from Havana to Key West, Florida.

B. Definitions. Match the definitions (1–7) to words from the box in **A**.

1. working by itself _____

2. the act of moving _____

3. related to the human mind _____

4. to make something better, improve it _____

5. to produce or cause something to begin _____

6. relating to your DNA _____

7. to move or change something slightly _____

Word Link The suffix **-ic** or **-atic** can be used to form an adjective, e.g., *genetic, photographic, problematic, automatic.*

VIEWING Living at High Altitude

Before You Watch

A. Matching. You will hear these words and phrases in the video. Match each word or phrase with its definition.

1. _____ mountain sickness
2. _____ hemoglobin
3. _____ altitude
4. _____ oxygen
5. _____ lungs

a. height above sea level
b. a colorless gas in the air that people and animals need to live
c. the two organs in your chest that fill with air when you breathe in
d. a medical problem caused by low air pressure at high places
e. the red substance in blood that carries oxygen around the body

B. Predict. Based on the title, the vocabulary, and the images below, what do you think the video will be about?

While You Watch

A. Sequencing. Number these high-altitude people from **1** to **3** in the order they are mentioned in the video. One group of people is not mentioned.

a. people in the Ethiopian Highlands

b. people in the Andes Mountains

c. people in the Rocky Mountains

d. people in the Himalaya Mountains

B. Summary Completion. Complete the summary of the video using words from the box.

biological	breathe	established	fire	lungs
oxygen	sickness	thicker	thinner	tools

Living in mountains

- air is **1.** _____
- people take in less **2.** _____
- cause of hypoxia

High Altitude Peoples

Mountain 3. _____ studies

Tibetans
- **4.** _____ faster
- get more oxygen into **5.** _____ and move it around quickly

Andean people
- have more hemoglobin in their blood (blood is **6.** _____)

Ethiopian highlanders
- scientists haven't yet **7.** _____ how they've adapted

Adaptations

Cultural
- need to make and take **8.** _____ with you
- need warm clothes, and **9.** _____ to make them

10. _____
- DNA studies may prove people are adapted to high altitudes

After You Watch

A. Discussion. Discuss these questions with a partner.

1. Have you ever been in a high-altitude place? How did you feel?
2. What other extreme environments have humans adapted to?

SKIN DEEP

A young Asaro mudman from Papua New Guinea: "Here," says scientist Nancy Sullivan, ". . . to be masculine is to be well made-up."

Warm Up

Discuss these questions with a partner.

1. What kinds of things or people would you describe as beautiful?

2. What do you think the expression "Beauty is only skin deep" means? Do you think it is true?

3. What do people in your country do to make themselves more beautiful?

A man of the Huli tribe from Papua New Guinea preparing for an annual festival called *sing-sing*.

Before You Read

A. Survey. Complete the survey about beauty. Then explain your answers to a partner.

	Yes.	No.
1. I spend a lot of time thinking about my appearance.		
2. I think good-looking people have easier lives than other people.		
3. I think it's fine for men to wear makeup.		
4. Women are judged on their looks more than men are.		
5. If I lost my hair, I might consider wearing a wig.		
6. Too many people diet to make themselves more attractive.		

B. Scan. Quickly scan the reading on pages 25–27. Match the people with their attitudes toward beauty.

People	What is considered attractive
1. _____ The ancient Maya	**a.** smaller noses and chins
2. _____ Most women	**b.** men with painted faces
3. _____ People of the Huli culture	**c.** cross-eyed people
4. _____ 18th-century French people	**d.** large shoulders and narrow waists
5. _____ Most men	**e.** large white wigs

WHAT IS BEAUTY?

> A trainee geisha puts on her makeup in Kyoto, Japan.

1   **THE SEARCH FOR BEAUTY** spans centuries and continents. Paintings of Egyptians dating back over 4,000 years show both men and women painting their nails and wearing makeup. On the other side of the globe, the ancient Maya of Central America considered crossed eyes[1] beautiful,
5   and hung little balls between children's eyes to develop this look. In 18th-century France, wealthy noblemen[2] wore large wigs of long white hair to make themselves attractive. In cultures throughout the world, people have gone to extreme lengths to achieve the goal of beauty.

Today, people continue to **devote** a lot of time and money to their
10   appearance. According to a recent report, one out of three consumers globally say they are spending more money today on beauty and health care products than ever before. Worldwide, sales of makeup, dieting, hair- and skin-care products, as well as gym memberships and cosmetic surgery,[3] generate billions of dollars every year.

15   And there is at least one good reason for the desire to be attractive: Beauty is power. Studies suggest that good-looking people make more money, get called on more often in class, and are perceived as friendlier.

---

1 **Crossed eyes** are eyes that seem to look toward each other.
2 **Noblemen** are men who belong to a high rank, title, or status.
3 **Cosmetic surgery** is surgery done to make someone look more attractive.

But what exactly *is* beauty? Trying to define it is difficult, and yet we know it when we see it—or so we think. "Beauty is health," says one psychologist. "It's a billboard saying 'I'm healthy. I can pass on your genes.'" And our awareness of it may start at a very early age. In one set of studies, six-month-old babies were shown a series of photographs. The faces in the pictures had been rated for attractiveness by a group of college students. In the studies, the babies spent more time looking at the attractive faces than the unattractive ones.

The idea that even babies judge appearance makes perfect sense to many researchers. In studies done by psychologists such as Victor Johnston at New Mexico State University and David Perrett at the University of St. Andrews in Scotland, men regularly showed a preference for women with certain features:

< Comédie Française
performers await their
entrance to a Molière
comedy, in Paris, France.

larger eyes, clear skin, fuller lips, and a smaller
nose and chin. Another study suggests that
40 women prefer men with large shoulders and
a narrow waist. According to scientists, the
mind unconsciously tells men and women that
these traits—the full lips, clear skin, strong
shoulders—equal health and genetic
45 well-being. In other words, it's a **fundamental**
part of human nature to look for these
qualities in a **mate**.

Not everyone agrees with this **notion**,
however. "Our hardwiredness can be **altered**
50 by all sorts of expectations—**predominantly**
cultural," says C. Loring Brace, an
anthropologist at the University of Michigan.
What is considered attractive in one culture
might not be in another. Look in most Western
55 fashion magazines, for example, and the
women on the pages are thin. But is this the
"perfect" body type for women worldwide?
Douglas Yu, a biologist from Great Britain,
and Glenn Shepard, an anthropologist at the
60 University of California at Berkeley, say no;
what is considered beautiful is **subjective** and
varies around the world. Yu and Shepard found
in one study, for example, that native peoples
in southeast Peru preferred shapes regarded as
65 overweight in Western cultures.

Take another example: In every culture, one's
hairstyle sends a clear message. In the Huli
culture of Papua New Guinea, men grow their
hair long as a symbol of health and strength.
70 Teenage boys in this culture learn from a
young age to style and decorate their hair—a
behavior more commonly associated with the
opposite **gender** in many cultures. It is also
the men in this culture who are the objects of
75 beauty. For certain festivals and celebrations,
men dress up and paint their faces. The more
colorful a man is, the more masculine[4]—and
attractive—he is considered.

For better or worse, beauty plays a role in
80 our lives. But it is extremely difficult to define
exactly what makes one person attractive to
another. Although there do seem to be certain
physical traits that are considered universally
appealing, it is also true that beauty does
85 not always **conform** to a single, **uniform**
standard. A person's cultural background, for
example, may influence what he or she finds
attractive in others. In the end, beauty really is,
as the saying goes, in the eye of the beholder.

---

4 **Masculine** qualities and things are typical for men,
in contrast to women.

Reading Comprehension

Multiple Choice. Choose the best answer for each question.

Gist

1. What is this reading mainly about?
   a. what people think about beauty
   b. the history of beauty
   c. the world's most beautiful people
   d. how beauty is power

Detail

2. The ancient Maya hung balls between children's eyes _____.
   a. because they hoped it would improve their eyesight
   b. to differentiate boys from girls
   c. because they thought crossed eyes were beautiful
   d. to add an attractive "third" eye

Vocabulary

3. In line 17, *perceived* can be replaced with _____.
   a. known
   b. seen
   c. treated
   d. compared

Detail

4. In paragraph 4 (starting line 18), the babies in the study _____.
   a. were shown photos of college students
   b. were entered in a beauty contest
   c. were rated for their beauty
   d. were able to tell attractive from unattractive faces

Detail

5. What determines the beauty of a Huli man in Papua New Guinea?
   a. how young he is
   b. how colorful he is
   c. how strong he is
   d. how big his mask is

Inference

6. What do you think the saying in the last sentence means?
   a. Beauty is subjective and is different for different people.
   b. Beauty is something that first appeals to sight.
   c. Beauty is something that is held in high esteem.
   d. Beauty of a person depends on their eyes.

Detail

7. According to the writer, perceptions of beauty _____.
   a. change over time
   b. are the same for every person
   c. have little influence on a person's success
   d. can be easily defined

Critical Thinking

Inferring: What do you think Brace means by "Our hardwiredness can be altered by all sorts of expectations"?

_____

Discussion: Do you agree with the saying "Beauty is in the eye of the beholder"? Give examples to support your opinion.

Using Examples to Support Claims

Usually when a writer makes a claim, it needs to be supported. One way to do this is by providing concrete examples. These may (but not always) be introduced with a phrase such as *for example, for instance, like,* and *such as.*

In the reading passage (on pages 25–27), the writer makes the claim that people continue to spend a lot of time and money on their appearance. This is supported by mentioning the increased sales of makeup, dieting, hair- and skin-care products, gym memberships, and cosmetic surgery.

Multiple Choice. Choose the best answer for each question.

1. Use of makeup in which culture is given as an example of the long history of beauty?
   a. Egypt
   b. the Maya
   c. Japan
   d. Papua New Guinea

2. Which of these is NOT given as an example of "Beauty is power"?
   a. Attractive people make more money.
   b. Attractive people get called on more often in class.
   c. Attractive people are seen as friendlier.
   d. Attractive people are perceived as more social.

3. According to the passage, which trait is an example of genetic well-being?
   a. clear skin
   b. strong teeth
   c. thin lips
   d. a full head of hair

4. The native Peruvian preference for heavier female body shapes is given as an example to illustrate what?
   a. that it's not necessary to spend a lot of money to be attractive
   b. that the notion of beauty never stops changing
   c. what is considered beautiful varies around the world
   d. that larger women in Peru are more beautiful than thinner women in the West

Vocabulary Practice

A. Completion. Complete the information using the correct form of words from the box. Two words are extra.

> | alter | conform | devote | fundamental |
> |-------|---------|--------|-------------|
> | gender | notion | predominantly | uniform |

Anita Roddick

Anita Roddick, founder of The Body Shop, was committed to the betterment of the world we live in. She was not prepared to **1.** _____ to business practices that she saw as destructive to the environment. Her beliefs in social and environmental responsibility were **2.** _____ to the way in which she established her own business, and led her to **3.** _____ her time and energy to raising awareness of the need to protect the environment. When Roddick died, Adrian Bellamy, chairman of Body Shop International, said that one of Roddick's achievements was to **4.** _____ the world of business. Roddick believed that the business world, traditionally, does things **5.** _____ for personal gain. However, she believed in the **6.** _____ that "business can and must be a force for positive social change."

∧ Anita Roddick
(1942–2007)

B. Completion. Complete the sentences using the correct form of words from the box. Two words are extra.

> | gender | mate | notion |
> |--------|------|--------|
> | predominant | subjective | uniform |

1. People don't have _____ ideas on what beauty is; opinions vary greatly.

2. Nowadays, in many places, people of both _____ buy and use cosmetics; it is not a practice restricted to women.

3. When looking for a _____, female peacocks are attracted by the male peacock's large, brightly colored tail.

4. Our ideas about beauty are highly _____, What one person finds attractive may be unattractive to another.

> **Usage** The word **uniform** can be used as a noun or an adjective. As a noun, it refers to a set of clothes, e.g., *a school uniform*; as an adjective, it means "even and regular throughout," e.g., *cut food into uniform shapes*.

SKIN:
THE BODY'S CANVAS[1]

A makeup artist prepares a model for Fashion Week in New York City, New York, U.S.A.

[1] **Canvas** is a strong, heavy cloth often used to do oil paintings on.

Before You Read

A. Discussion. In what ways is skin important to us? Make a list with a partner.

_____

_____

_____

_____

B. Scan. Quickly scan the reading on pages 32–33. Match each practice with a place in the world where it takes place.

Place	Practice
1. _____ New Zealand	**a.** full-body tattoos
2. _____ Japan	**b.** scarring (cutting or burning the skin)
3. _____ West Africa	**c.** full-facial tattoos

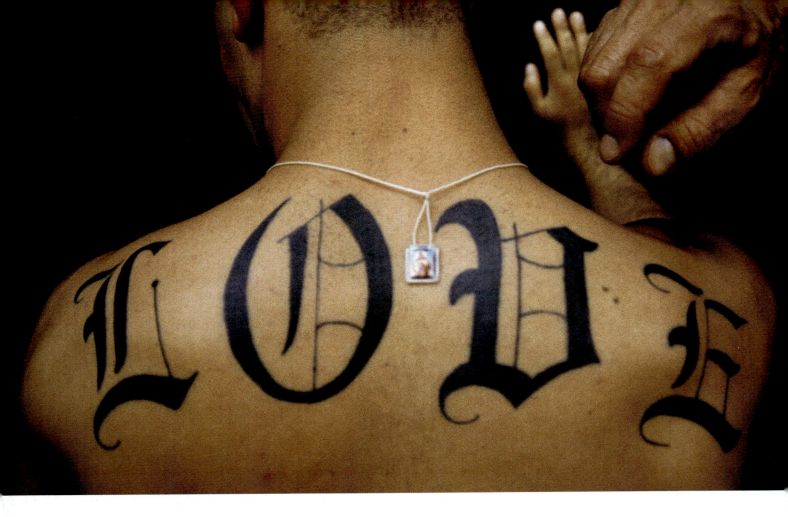

∧ The word *love* tattooed on a man's back

Protection and Color

If you took off your skin and laid it flat, it would cover an area of about 1.9 square meters (21 square feet), making it by far the body's largest organ. Covering almost the entire body, skin protects us from a variety of **external** forces, such as extremes of temperature, damaging sunlight, harmful **chemicals**, and dangerous infections. Skin is also packed with nerves, which keeps the brain in touch with the outside world.

The health of our skin and its ability to perform its protective functions are **crucial** to our well-being. However, the appearance of our skin is equally—if not more—important to many people on this planet.

Take skin color, for example. Your genes determine your skin's color, but for centuries, humans have tried to lighten or darken their skin in an attempt to be more attractive. In the 1800s, white skin was desirable for many Europeans. Skin this color meant that its owner was a member of the upper class and did not have to work in the sun. Among darker-skinned people in some parts of the world, products used to lighten skin are still popular today. In other cultures during the 20th century, as cities grew and work moved indoors, attitudes toward light skin shifted in the opposite direction. Tanned skin began to indicate **leisure** time and health. In many places today, suntanning on the beach or in a salon[2] remains popular, even though people are more aware of the dangers of UV rays.[3]

---

2 A **salon** is a place where people have their hair cut or colored, or have beauty treatments.

3 **UV rays** (or **ultraviolet rays**) are what cause your skin to become darker in color after having been in sunlight.

Identity and Status

35 Just as people have altered their skin's color to **denote** wealth and beauty, so too have cultures around the globe marked their skin to indicate cultural **identity** or community status. Tattooing, for example, has been

40 carried out for thousands of years. Leaders in places including ancient Egypt, Britain, and Peru wore tattoos to mark their status, or their bravery. Today, among the Maori people of New Zealand as well as in cultures in Samoa,

45 Tahiti, and Borneo, full-facial tattoos are still used to identify the wearer as a member of a certain family and to symbolize the person's achievements in life.

In Japan, tattooing has been practiced since

50 around the fifth century B.C. The government made tattooing illegal in 1870, and though there are no laws against it today, tattoos are still strongly associated with **criminals**—particularly the *yakuza*, or the Japanese mafia,[4]

55 who are known for their full-body tattoos. The complex design of a yakuza member's tattoo usually includes symbols of character traits that the wearer wants to have. The process of getting a full-body tattoo is both slow and

60 painful and can take up to two years to complete.

In some cultures, scarring—a marking caused by cutting or burning the skin—is practiced, usually among people who have darker skin

65 on which a tattoo would be difficult to see. For many men in West Africa, for instance, scarring is a rite of passage—an act that symbolizes that a male has **matured** from a child into an adult. In Australia, among some native peoples, cuts

70 are made on the skin of both men and women when they reach 16 or 17. Without these, members were traditionally not permitted to trade, sing ceremonial songs, or participate in other activities.

75 Not all skin markings are **permanent**, though. In countries such as Morocco and India, women decorate their skin with colorful henna designs for celebrations such as weddings and important religious holidays. The henna coloring,

80 which comes from a plant, **fades** and disappears over time.

In recent years in many industrialized nations,[5] tattooing, henna body art, and, to a lesser degree, scarring, have been gaining in popularity.

85 What makes these practices appealing to those living in modern cities? According to photographer Chris Rainier, whose book *Ancient Marks* examines body markings around the globe, people are looking for a connection with

90 the traditional world. "There is a whole sector of modern society—people in search of identity, people in search of meaning . . . ," says Rainier. "Hence, [there has been] a huge explosion of tattooing and body marking . . . [I]t's . . .

95 mankind wanting identity, wanting a sense of place . . . and a sense of culture within their community."

---

4 The **mafia** is a criminal organization that makes money illegally.

5 An **industrialized nation** is a country that has a lot of industry, such as factories, businesses, etc.

The scars on the face of a Gobir woman from Niger indicate her membership in the tribe.

Reading Comprehension

Multiple Choice. Choose the best answer for each question.

1. What is this reading mainly about?
   a. the skin's role in our overall health
   b. the ways people change the appearance of their skin
   c. the different reasons people get tattoos
   d. cultural ceremonies that involve skin tattooing

2. What can we infer about the tattoos of the Maori?
   a. Only men get facial tattoos.
   b. Members of the same family have similar facial tattoos.
   c. No one gets their entire face tattooed anymore.
   d. Both men and women get facial tattoos but never body tattoos.

3. Why are tattoos disapproved of in Japanese society?
   a. They are often associated with crime.
   b. They are painful.
   c. They take too long to complete.
   d. They are illegal.

4. In West Africa, what is done to mark a male child's reaching of adulthood?
   a. tanning
   b. tattooing
   c. scarring
   d. skin whitening

5. In line 71, what does *these* refer to?
   a. scars
   b. customs
   c. males
   d. celebrations

6. What is NOT true about henna designs?
   a. They are used to celebrate religious holidays.
   b. Some brides decorate their skin with them.
   c. They are permanent.
   d. They are made with plants.

7. In line 93, the word *explosion* can be replaced with _____.
   a. bombing
   b. destruction
   c. increase
   d. decrease

Critical Thinking

Relating: The passage gives an example of a rite of passage. Can you think of any other examples in your own culture?

_____

Discussion: What are some other ways that people in your culture express individual identity? How do you?

Determining the Main Idea of Paragraphs

While it's important to have an overall understanding of a reading, it's equally important to be able to determine the main idea of each paragraph of the reading. You should read the first line of the paragraph and then quickly skim the rest. Some paragraphs also have headings; these headings often tell you what the main idea is.

Understanding the main idea of each paragraph can be especially useful when taking notes, or when creating a summary outline or word web of the reading.

⌄ In many cultures, henna is traditionally used for special occasions, such as birthdays and weddings.

Multiple Choice. Look back at the reading on pages 32–33. What is each paragraph's main idea? Choose the correct answer.

1. **Paragraph 1**
   a. the importance of skin
   b. how to have healthy skin

2. **Paragraph 2**
   a. the role our skin plays in our overall health
   b. the importance of skin health and appearance

3. **Paragraph 3**
   a. reasons for and ways of changing skin color
   b. skin tanning as a symbol of leisure time and health

4. **Paragraph 4**
   a. the history of facial tattooing
   b. cultural reasons for tattooing

5. **Paragraph 5**
   a. how tattoos are viewed in Japan
   b. how tattooing has changed in Japan

6. **Paragraph 6**
   a. reasons for scarring the skin
   b. scarring as a rite of passage in West Africa

7. **Paragraph 7**
   a. an example of non-permanent skin marking
   b. henna in Morocco

8. **Paragraph 8**
   a. body marking as an ancient phenomenon
   b. body marking as a means of identity in modern society

Vocabulary Practice

A. Completion. Complete the information using the correct form of words from the box. Four words are extra.

chemical	criminal	crucial	denote	external
fade	identity	leisure	maturity	permanent

Tattooing was traditionally a(n) **1.** _____
part of life for members of the Iban tribe of Sarawak, Malaysia.
Iban tattooing was a spiritual art form, and it was believed
to have powers of protecting the Iban people from harm and
disease. Tattoos were also used to **2.** _____
the wearer's skills and cultural **3.** _____.

Originally, the tattooing was done using ancient recipes
involving natural dyes from plants and traditional wooden
tools. The dyes were **4.** _____ and could
not be removed. Newly done Iban tattoos look dark, but
they gradually **5.** _____ somewhat from
sunlight, or as the dye is absorbed into the skin. Today, for the
Iban people, Western tattoos are more popular than traditional
designs, and modern tattooing machines are used. Modern
6. _____ dyes have mainly replaced the
plant-based ones.

B. Words in Context. Use words from the box in **A** to complete
the definitions.

1. A person who breaks the law is a(n)

   _____.

2. A(n) _____ activity is one you enjoy
   doing when you are not working.

3. If something is _____, it lasts forever.

4. If something is on the outside rather than the inside, it is

   _____.

5. Your _____ is your distinct personality
   or who you are.

6. A person's _____ can be measured by
   his or her physical and mental development.

∧ An Iban man showing
off his traditional tattoos

> **Word Link** The
> letters **-al** at the end
> of a word often mean
> that the word is an
> adjective, e.g., *chemical,
> external, crucial.*

VIEWING Skin Mask

Before You Watch

A. Labeling. You will hear these words in the video. Use the words to complete the picture captions in **B**.

eyebrows	lashes	masks	silicone

B. Sequencing. What do you think are the steps involved in making a face mask? Number the steps in order (**1–4**).

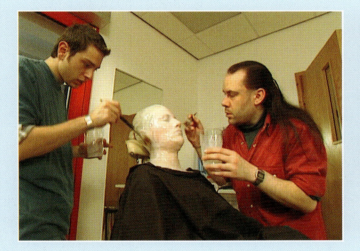

a. The face is painted in _____.

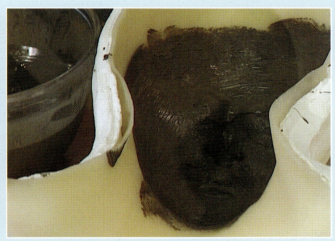

b. Positive and negative _____ are created.

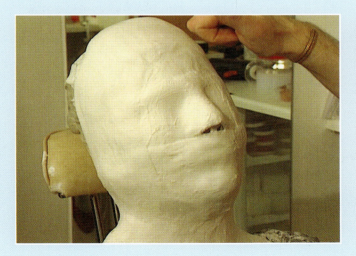

c. The face is wrapped.

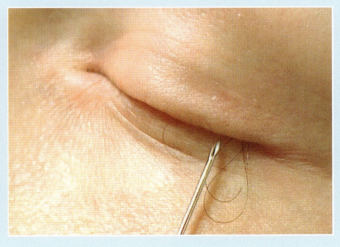

d. _____ and _____ are added.

While You Watch

A. Sequencing. Look back at page 37 and check your guesses. Re-number any steps.

B. True or False. Mark the sentences **T** (True) or **F** (False).

1. Silicone is a rubberlike material.   **T**   **F**
2. Silicone prevents eyebrows and lashes from sticking.   **T**   **F**
3. It takes about an hour for the silicone to dry.   **T**   **F**
4. The model's mask is compared to a living mummy's mask.   **T**   **F**
5. It can take up to three hours to add one eyebrow.   **T**   **F**
6. The finished mask has both the look and feel of real skin.   **T**   **F**

After You Watch

A. Discussion. Discuss these questions with a partner.

1. What do you think the masks are used for?

2. What part of the mask-making process do you think is the most difficult for the artists? Which is the most difficult for the model?

∧ Model Cassandra Wheatley holds a silicone mask of her face.

ANIMALS IN DANGER

A black rhino is airlifted to a new habitat from Ithala Game Reserve, South Africa.

Warm Up

Discuss these questions with a partner.

1. What animals can you think of that are endangered?

2. What are some of the reasons animals become endangered?

3. Do you think that it is important for humans to protect endangered species? Why or why not?

39

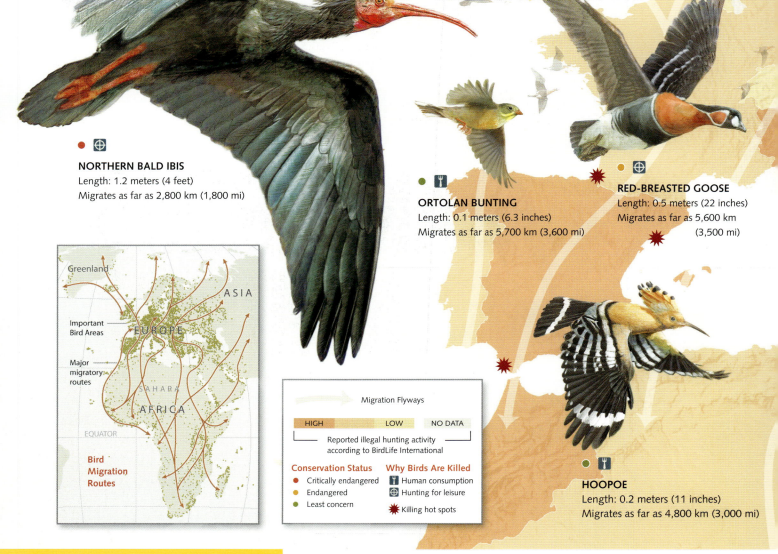

NORTHERN BALD IBIS
Length: 1.2 meters (4 feet)
Migrates as far as 2,800 km (1,800 mi)

ORTOLAN BUNTING
Length: 0.1 meters (6.3 inches)
Migrates as far as 5,700 km (3,600 mi)

RED-BREASTED GOOSE
Length: 0.5 meters (22 inches)
Migrates as far as 5,600 km
(3,500 mi)

HOOPOE
Length: 0.2 meters (11 inches)
Migrates as far as 4,800 km (3,000 mi)

Greenland
ASIA
Important
Bird Areas
EUROPE
Major
migratory
routes
SAHARA
AFRICA
EQUATOR
**Bird
Migration
Routes**

Migration Flyways

| HIGH | LOW | NO DATA |

Reported illegal hunting activity
according to BirdLife International

Conservation Status
● Critically endangered
● Endangered
● Least concern

Why Birds Are Killed
🍴 Human consumption
⊕ Hunting for leisure
✹ Killing hot spots

Before You Read

A. Discussion. Use the information above to answer the questions.

1. What countries and regions do the birds cross?
2. Which of the birds shown travels the longest distance?
3. Why are they being killed?

B. Skim. Look quickly at the reading on pages 41–43. Which questions do you expect the passage to answer? Check (✓) your answers. Then read the passage to check your ideas.

☐ What's killing these birds?
☐ How does the weather affect bird migration?[1]
☐ Why do some birds migrate and others don't?
☐ What are people doing to save the birds?

1 **Migration** is the movement from one place to another.

RED-BACKED SHRIKE
Length: 0.1 meters (7 inches)
Migrates as far as 10,900 km (6,800 mi)

SAKER FALCON
Length: 1 to 1.2 meters (3.5 to 4 feet)
Migrates as far as 4,000 km (2,500 mi)

DANGEROUS JOURNEY

1　**IT'S AN ASTOUNDING FEAT:** Every summer, three billion birds of some 300 species—songbirds, waterbirds, and many others—migrate from northern Africa to Europe and Asia. In the winter, they return to Africa's warmer shores. As they travel from one
5　place to another, they navigate using the sun, the stars, smells, and land forms to help them find their way.

Both large and small birds travel thousands of kilometers, often stopping at **locations** along the way to rest. In late fall in the northern hemisphere, for example, golden orioles fly from
10　northern to southern Europe, and then cross the Mediterranean Sea into Africa. The birds often stop at different oases[2] in northern Africa before flying almost 1,600 kilometers (over 1,000 miles) across the Sahara Desert and then on to central and southern Africa.

---

2 An **oasis** (*plural: oases*) is a small area in a desert that has water and plants.

"There are no birds. We walk for hours without seeing any. It's really scary."

15 The birds' migration is long and difficult, and some of the animals **inevitably** die during each trip. However, it is not this twice-a-year journey that **poses** the greatest risk to these animals. The main threat to the birds' survival comes from
20 human hunters. All over the Mediterranean, millions of migrating birds are killed for food, profit, and sport every year. As a result, bird populations are dropping all over the region.

In nations along the Mediterranean, many
25 migratory birds are illegally **trapped** or shot. In addition to traps, hunters also use electronic calls to catch birds. This tool, which a hunter can operate from a cell phone, mimics bird sounds and is very **effective** in attracting the
30 animals—so effective that in some countries, bird populations have plummeted. "There are no birds," says one Albanian man. "We walk for hours without seeing any. It's really scary." Some hunters also use nets to capture birds as they fly
35 close to the sea. The nets are high—going from ground level to just over 3 meters (11 feet)— and invisible to the birds, allowing hunters to trap hundreds of birds at a time.

Working for Change

40 Countries all over the Mediterranean are aware that bird populations are in danger, and many are working to address this problem. In the European Union, hunting migratory birds is illegal in some countries, while in others, it
45 is **strictly** controlled—the birds can only be hunted at a certain time of year. This hasn't completely stopped bird poaching[3] in Europe, but more nature-protection groups are making sure that laws are obeyed. The organization

50 WWF[4] Italy, for example, works with volunteers to stop poachers and destroy birdsong devices that attract birds. This has been successful in many places throughout the country. Sicily, for example, was once a
55 hot spot[5] for illegal bird hunting. Today, it has mostly **eliminated** poaching, and bird-watching is becoming popular on the island.

Across the Mediterranean, another group— Nature Conservation Egypt—is working to
60 increase protection of its country's natural scenery and wildlife, including its migratory birds. As part of a **current** project, the organization is trying to promote activities such as eco-tourism along the coasts. The
65 hope is that, as more tourists come to visit protected natural areas, there will be an **incentive** to care for the birds and their habitats. If this happens, say conservationists, bird populations will quickly return to normal.

70 Wildlife organizations around the Mediterranean are helping to bring about change. Hunting **bans** are working, says Martin Schneider-Jacoby, a bird specialist for the German organization EuroNatur. But there
75 is still more to do. Conservationists hope to stop hunting and restore bird habitats all over the Mediterranean. If this can be done, the birds' numbers will increase. There's a long way to go, Schneider-Jacoby says, but like an
80 oasis in the desert after a long journey, there is hope.

---

3 **Poaching** is the illegal hunting and killing of animals.
4 **WWF** stands for World Wide Fund for Nature.
5 A **hot spot** is a place where something happens regularly.

Golden orioles feeding a nest of hungry chicks, in Beibrza National Park, Poland

Reading Comprehension

Multiple Choice. Choose the best answer for each question.

Gist

1. This reading is mainly about _____.
   a. problems caused by migrating birds
   b. how birds are being hunted worldwide
   c. how tourism is causing a drop in bird population
   d. dangers to migrating birds in the Mediterranean

Purpose

2. The purpose of the first paragraph is to describe _____.
   a. how many birds travel large distances to and from Africa
   b. why some birds migrate while others do not
   c. why bird numbers are starting to drop in the Mediterranean
   d. how migrating birds are able to use stars as a tool for navigation

Detail

3. What is the biggest danger to migrating birds?
   a. crossing the Sahara Desert
   b. lack of food
   c. being hunted by humans
   d. storms in the Mediterranean

Detail

4. Which of these is NOT mentioned as a way of attracting and catching birds?
   a. traps
   b. offering food
   c. nets
   d. bird calls

Cause and Effect

5. Why has bird-watching become popular in Sicily?
   a. The weather has changed and become more pleasant.
   b. There is now very little poaching of birds.
   c. Some extremely rare birds have been seen in Sicily.
   d. Birdsong devices are attracting more birds to the area.

Detail

6. What is Nature Conservation Egypt doing to protect the birds?
   a. eliminating hunting
   b. promoting eco-tourism
   c. banning birdsong devices
   d. allowing hunting only at a certain time

Inference

7. Which of these statements would Martin Schneider-Jacoby probably agree with the most?
   a. More countries need to ban hunting to restore bird numbers.
   b. It's likely that bird populations will continue to decrease.
   c. There needs to be more protection of desert oases.
   d. The only way to increase bird populations is to allow limited hunting.

Critical Thinking

Inferring: Do you think the writer is generally negative or positive about the future for migrating birds? Give examples from the passage to support your answer.

Discussion: Can you think of any other animals in your country that are facing similar dangers? Is anything being done to protect them?

Guessing the Meaning of Unfamiliar Words

When you come across an unfamiliar word, you can sometimes guess its meaning by looking at its context—the words and sentences around it. First, determine the word's part of speech. Then look to see if there are synonyms, antonyms, or examples in the sentence that can help you determine its meaning. For example, read the sentence below.

*Most large birds kill and eat their own prey, but the **condor** prefers to eat a **carcass**.*

We may not know the meaning of the nouns *condor* and *carcass*. However, from the context, we can determine that a condor is a type of large bird, and that a carcass is an animal that has already died.

A. **Noticing.** Look back at the reading on pages 41–43. Find and underline the words in **bold** below (1–8).

B. **Analyzing.** Now look at the context around each of the eight words in the reading. Choose the option below (a–d) that is closest in meaning to each word.

1. **astounding** (paragraph 1)
   a. true   b. common   c. amazing   d. strange

2. **navigate** (paragraph 1)
   a. find a route   b. stop on land   c. look ahead   d. stay warm

3. **threat** (paragraph 3)
   a. friend   b. journey   c. knowledge   d. danger

4. **mimics** (paragraph 4)
   a. destroys   b. imagines   c. copies   d. telephones

5. **plummeted** (paragraph 4)
   a. decreased slowly   c. decreased quickly
   b. increased slowly   d. increased quickly

6. **obeyed** (paragraph 5)
   a. considered   b. followed   c. changed   d. ignored

7. **devices** (paragraph 5)
   a. birds   b. areas   c. tools   d. hunters

8. **bring about** (paragraph 7)
   a. ask for   b. deal with   c. lead to   d. move around

Vocabulary Practice

A. Completion. Complete the information using the words from the box. Two words are extra.

ban	current	effective	eliminated
locations	posed	strictly	trap

For decades, habitat loss and hunting **1.** _____ a huge threat to the whooping cranes of North America. When the whooping crane was listed as endangered in 1967, there were just 48 birds left in the wild.

In 1978, whooping crane habitat was established in several U.S. states. They now nest in three **2.** _____: Wisconsin, Florida, and at Wood Buffalo National Park in Canada. Due to nest protection, **3.** _____ breeding and reproduction programs, and a(n) **4.** _____ on hunting that is **5.** _____ enforced, the **6.** _____ population of North America's tallest bird is now at about 600 birds. Though the crane's future remains uncertain, it is one of conservation's great success stories.

B. Words in Context. Complete the sentences using the correct form of words from the box. One word is extra.

effective	eliminate	incentive	inevitable	pose	trap

1. If something is _____, it is certain to happen.

2. A(n) _____ strategy is one that works well.

3. A law that _____ poaching, gets rid of it.

4. An animal that is _____ is caught and cannot get away.

5. A(n) _____ to do something encourages you to do it.

∧ Conservation efforts have led to a limited recovery of the whooping crane, the tallest North American bird.

Word Link The suffix **-ive** meaning "having the quality of" can be added to some words to make adjectives, e.g., *effective, creative, productive, attractive, expensive.*

TRACKING THE SNOW LEOPARD

Before You Read

A. Quiz. How much do you know about snow leopards?
Read the sentences below and circle **T** (True) or **F** (False).
Then read the captions on pages 47–51 to check your answers.

1. They live in eastern and southern Africa.   **T**   **F**
2. When hunting, they can leap up to several meters.   **T**   **F**
3. They are most active at dawn and dusk.   **T**   **F**
4. They live in mountainous regions.   **T**   **F**

B. Skim. Quickly skim the passage on pages 48–51.
Check (✓) the information that the writer discusses.
Then read the passage to check your ideas.

- [ ] methods of protecting snow leopards
- [ ] how young snow leopards survive in the wild
- [ ] conflicts between snow leopards and herders

∧ Snow leopards live at elevations between 3,000 and 5,000 meters (9,800–17,000 feet) in the mountains of Central Asia. They are perfectly adapted to a cold and dry habitat.

1 **"WHEN A SNOW LEOPARD STALKS** its prey among the mountain walls, it moves . . . softly, slowly," explains Indian biologist Raghunandan Singh Chundawat, who has studied the animal for
5 years. "If it knocks a stone loose, it will reach out a foot to stop it from falling and making noise." One might be moving right now, perfectly silent, maybe close by. But where? And how many are left to see?

10 Best known for its spotted coat and long **distinctive** tail, the snow leopard is one of the world's most secretive animals. These elusive[1] cats can only be found high in the remote, mountainous regions of Central Asia. For this
15 reason, and because they hunt primarily at night, they are very rarely seen.

Snow leopards have been officially protected since 1975, but **enforcing** this law has proven difficult. Many continue to be killed for their
20 fur and body parts, which are worth a fortune on the black market.[2] In recent years, though, **conflict** with local herders has also led to a number of snow leopard deaths. This is because the big cats kill the herders' animals, and
25 **drag** the bodies away to eat high up in the mountains.

---

1 Something that is **elusive** is difficult to find.

2 If something is bought or sold on the **black market**, it is bought or sold illegally.

A snow leopard will reach out a foot to stop a falling stone from making noise.

< When hunting, snow leopards have been known to leap more than 9 meters (30 feet), six times their body length.

As a result of these pressures, the current snow leopard population is estimated at only 4,000 to 7,000, and some fear that the actual number may already have dropped below 3,500. The only way to **reverse** this trend and bring these cats back from near extinction, say conservationists, is to make them more valuable alive than dead.

Because farming is difficult in Central Asia's cold, dry **landscape**, traditional cultures depend mostly on livestock (mainly sheep and goats) to survive in these mountainous regions. At night, when snow leopards hunt, herders' animals are in danger of snow leopard attacks. If a family loses even a few animals, it can push them into desperate **poverty**. "The wolf[3] comes and kills, eats, and goes somewhere else," said one herder, "but snow leopards are always around. They have killed one or two animals many times . . . Everybody wanted to finish this leopard."

_____

3 A **wolf** is a wild animal that looks like a large dog.

To address this problem, local religious leaders have called for an end to snow leopard killings, saying that these wild animals have the right to exist peacefully. They've also tried to convince people that the leopards are quite rare, and thus it is important to protect them.

Financial incentives are also helping to slow snow leopard killings. The organization Snow Leopard Conservancy–India has established Himalayan Homestays, a program that sends visitors to herders' houses. For a clean room and bed, meals with the family, and an introduction to their culture, visitors pay about ten U.S. dollars a night. If guests come once every two weeks through the tourist season, the herders will earn enough income to replace the animals lost to snow leopards. In addition, the organization helps herders build protective fences that keep out snow leopards. It also conducts environmental classes at village schools, and trains the organization's members as nature guides, available for hire. In exchange, the herders agree not to kill snow leopards.

In Mongolia, a project called Snow Leopard Enterprises (SLE) helps herder communities earn extra money in exchange for their promise to protect the endangered cat.

Snow leopards are most active at dawn or dusk, but are rarely seen in the wild. They prefer to live and hunt alone, only pairing up during mating season.

Women in Mongolian herder communities make a variety of products—yarn for making clothes, decorative floor rugs, and toys—using the wool from their herds. SLE buys these items from herding families and sells them abroad. Herders must agree to protect the snow leopards and to encourage neighbors to do the same.

The arrangement increases herders' incomes by 10 to 15 percent, and elevates the **status** of the women. If no one in the community kills the protected animals over the course of a year, the program members are rewarded with a 20 percent **bonus** in addition to the money they've already made. An independent review in 2006 found no snow leopard killings in areas where SLE operates. Today, the organization continues to add more communities.

Projects like the Homestays program in India and SLE's business in Mongolia are doing well. Though they cover only a small part of the snow leopard's homeland, they make the leopards more valuable to more people each year. If these programs continue to do well, the snow leopard may just have a fighting chance.

Reading Comprehension

Multiple Choice. Choose the best answer for each question.

Main Idea

1. What is the main idea of the third paragraph (starting line 17)?
   a. Local herders are uncooperative in attempts to save snow leopards.
   b. The snow leopard's endangerment is due in part to the black market.
   c. Snow leopards are killed for their fur and body parts.
   d. It is difficult to enforce the laws made to protect the snow leopard.

Reference

2. In line 25, the word *bodies* refers to _____.
   a. the big cats
   b. snow leopards
   c. local herders
   d. the herders' animals

Reference

3. In line 31, *this trend* refers to _____.
   a. the fall in the snow leopard population
   b. the pressures caused by the black market
   c. increasing conflict with the herders
   d. the opinions of conservationists

Detail

4. According to conservationists, what's the best way to save the snow leopard?
   a. Create a nature park where they can be free.
   b. Move herders away from where the snow leopard lives.
   c. Pass laws to punish people who kill snow leopards for their fur.
   d. Make people recognize the value of living snow leopards.

Vocabulary

5. In line 48, the word *address* can be replaced with _____.
   a. solve
   b. locate
   c. discuss
   d. change

Detail

6. Which of these is NOT true about the Himalayan Homestays program?
   a. The organization helps herders to build fences.
   b. Herders provide accommodations to guests.
   c. Some herders work as nature guides.
   d. Visitors pay $10 a week to stay at a herder's house.

Detail

7. Why is the Mongolian women's status in the community "elevated" (paragraph 9)?
   a. They can encourage their neighbors.
   b. They are saving money for the snow leopards.
   c. They are earning money for the community.
   d. They are living higher up in the mountain.

Critical Thinking

Inferring: Do you think the writer is generally positive or negative about Himalayan Homestays and SLE? Why do you think so?

Discussion: Do you think keeping endangered animals in zoos or parks is a good way to save the species?

Understanding Conditional Relationships

Conditional sentences express an action and its consequences. A conditional sentence expresses a situation or an action (the main clause) that depends on certain conditions (the dependent clause). The condition is normally signaled by *if* or *when*. Note that the main clause (underlined below) can come first or last. Below are a few examples of conditional sentences.

If a jaguar is hungry, <u>it eats almost anything</u>.

<u>A jaguar can survive in an area of about 4.8 kilometers in diameter</u> if food is plentiful.

When food is scarce, <u>a jaguar will hunt over an area of 500 square kilometers</u>.

A. Matching. Match the clauses to make four sentences about tigers.

Condition

1. When a tiger lives in a zoo, _____
2. If a tiger is injured, _____
3. If a tiger breeds with a lion, _____
4. When a male tiger comes across another male tiger in its territory, _____

Main Clause

a. it's more likely to become a man-eater.

b. it can live five years longer than in the wild.

c. it gives birth to animals known as tigons or ligers.

d. it will usually threaten it.

B. Completion. Look back at the reading on pages 48–51, and answer the questions.

1. What will a snow leopard do if it knocks a stone loose while stalking prey?

   _____

2. What can happen if a herding family loses even a few of their animals?

   _____

3. How will herders benefit if guests come to stay during the tourist season?

   _____

4. In Mongolia, how is the community rewarded if no one kills a snow leopard in a year?

   _____

5. If Homestays and SLE continue to do well, what may happen?

   _____

A. Matching. Read the information below and match the correct form of each word in **red** with its definition.

The cheetah, an expert hunter, sits silently and scans for the perfect prey. Finding a target, it slowly **stalks** the animal until it is close enough to get its reward.

The cheetah is perfectly built for the kill. Its coloring allows it to disappear into the **landscape** to avoid being seen. And its speed allows it to chase its target. Once the prey is killed, the cheetah **drags** the animal to a safe place.

However, declining cheetah numbers mean that the animal's **status** is now vulnerable. To **reverse** the trend, game wardens are working to **enforce** the anti-poaching laws that should protect cheetah populations. It will be a sad day if this beautiful animal disappears from our planet.

1. to follow something in order to catch or kill it

   _____

2. to pull a heavy weight across the ground

   _____

3. to make something the opposite of what it is

   _____

4. to make sure people obey rules

   _____

5. the broad view that can be seen around you in the countryside

   _____

6. the state or condition of something at a particular time

   _____

∧ A cheetah and a vulture fight over prey in Serengeti National Park, Tanzania.

B. Words in Context. Complete each sentence with the correct answer.

1. Someone who lives in **poverty** _____.
   a. is in poor health   b. doesn't have enough money

2. **Conflict** between two countries may result in _____ between them.
   a. war   b. increased trade

3. Workers who receive a **bonus** are usually _____.
   a. pleased   b. displeased

4. If something is **distinctive** it is easily _____.
   a. recognizable   b. forgotten

> **Usage** As a noun, *conflict* refers to a serious disagreement. The stress is on the first syllable. As a verb, it means "to come into opposition" or "to differ," with the stress on the second syllable.

Tree Climber

A. Completion. You will hear these words in the video. Use the words to complete the information below.

branch	jaws	predator	prey

The leopard is a quiet and deadly nighttime **1.** _____. This leopard
is holding its **2.** _____—an impala—in its powerful
3. _____, while standing on a tree **4.** _____
in Mala Mala Game Reserve, South Africa.

B. Discussion. What do you know about leopards? Discuss these questions with a partner.

   1. Where do leopards live?

   2. What animals do leopards eat?

   3. What predators, if any, are a threat to leopards?

While You Watch

A. Sequencing. Put the events in order from **1** to **8**, and fill in the blanks with the correct answer.

- ☐ The _____ kills another impala.
- ☐ The lioness tries to climb a tree but can't.
- ☐ Another hyena tries to steal the impala.
- ☐ The leopard finishes its meal.
- ☐ A _____ arrives.
- 6 The hyena runs away.
- 7 A leopard kills an _____.
- ☐ A hyena runs away with the impala.

B. Completion. Circle the correct word or phrase to complete each caption.

a. Leopards spend more time in trees than any other (**animal / big cat**).

b. Relative to their weight, hyenas have the strongest (**jaws / legs**) in the reserve.

c. The hardest part for a leopard is (**killing its prey / deciding which branch will support the weight**).

d. The lion doesn't get the leopard's prey because the lion is too (**slow / heavy**).

After You Watch

A. Discussion. Discuss these questions with a partner.

1. From what you have learned in this unit, in what ways are leopards and snow leopards similar, and different?

2. Which of the animals featured in this unit do you think is most deserving of protection? Give reasons for your answer.

4

VIOLENT EARTH

A tornado sweeps across the open country in Oklahoma, U.S.A.

Warm Up

Discuss these questions with a partner.

1. What kinds of natural disasters can you think of?

2. Do natural disasters occur in your country?

3. Have any natural disasters been in the news recently?

Before You Read

A. Definitions. Read the caption on this page and match the words in **bold** with their definitions below.

1. used to describe a volcano that could erupt at any time _____
2. (for a volcano) threw out melted rock and smoke _____
3. sending people away from a dangerous place _____
4. the gray or black powder that is left after something burns

   _____
5. the top of a mountain _____
6. believed to have a connection to God, and given respect _____

B. Predict. Look quickly at the title, headings, and captions on pages 59–61. Which two volcanoes are discussed in the passage?

_____

Check (✓) the information you think you'll read about them.

☐ beliefs about the volcanoes

☐ why scientists are concerned about the volcanoes

☐ the size of the volcanoes

☐ other natural disasters in the two countries

∧ Indonesia is home to many **active** volcanoes, including Mt. Bromo (the **summit** is in the distance). Many Indonesians believe the volcanoes are **sacred**. In 2011, Mt. Bromo **erupted**, sending smoke and **ash** into the air. The area was prepared for **evacuation**.

SACRED MOUNTAINS

1 **VOLCANOES ARE BOTH CREATORS AND DESTROYERS.** They can shape lands and cultures, but can also cause great destruction and loss of life. Two of the best-known
5 examples are found at opposite ends of the world, separated by the Pacific Ring of Fire.

Japan's Sacred Summit

It's almost sunrise near the summit of Japan's Mount Fuji. Exhausted climbers, many of
10 whom have hiked the 3,776 meters (12,388 feet) through the night to reach this point, stop to watch as the sun begins its ascent,[1] spreading its golden rays across the mountain. For everyone, this is an important moment:
15 They have **witnessed** the **dawn** on Mount Fuji—the highest point in the Land of the Rising Sun.[2]

Located in the center of Japan, Mount Fuji (whose name means "without equal") is a
20 sacred site. Japan's native religion, Shintoism, considers Fuji a **holy** place. Other people believe the mountain and its waters have the power to make a sick person well. For many, climbing Fuji is also a rite of passage.
25 Some do it as part of a religious journey; for others, it is a test of strength. Whatever their reason, reaching the top in order to stand on Fuji's summit at sunrise is a must for many Japanese—and every July and August, almost
30 400,000 people attempt to do so.

---

1 An **ascent** is an upward movement.
2 Japan is sometimes also referred to as the **Land of the Rising Sun**.

Climbers normally begin ➤ their ascent of Mount Fuji around noon so they can stand at the top of Japan's highest mountain at sunrise the next morning.

Fuji is more than a sacred site and tourist destination, however. It is also an active volcano around which four million people have settled, and sits just 112 kilometers
35 (70 miles) from the crowded streets of Tokyo. The last time Fuji exploded, in 1707, it sent out a cloud of ash that covered the capital city and darkened the skies for weeks.

Today, new data have some volcanologists
40 concerned that Fuji may soon erupt again. According to Motoo Ukawa and his associates at the National Research Institute for Earth Science and **Disaster** Prevention, there has been an increase in activity under Fuji recently,
45 which may be caused by low-frequency

earthquakes. Understanding what causes these quakes may help scientists predict when Fuji, the largest of Japan's 86 active volcanoes, will come back to life. In the meantime, locals living near
50 Fuji hold special festivals each year to offer gifts to the goddess of the volcano—as they have for generations—so that she will not erupt and destroy the land and its people below.

Mexico's Smoking Mountain

55 Halfway across the globe from Fuji, Popocatépetl—one of the world's tallest and most dangerous active volcanoes—stands just 60 kilometers (37 miles) southeast of Mexico City. Although the volcano (whose name means

"What we're trying to learn are the symptoms signaling that El Popo will erupt."

Carlos Valdés González

60 "smoking mountain") has erupted many times over the centuries, scientists believe its last great eruption occurred around 820 A.D. In recent years, however, El Popo, as Mexicans call the mountain, has been
65 threatening to explode once more; in December 2000, almost 26,000 people were evacuated when El Popo started to send out ash and smoke. As with all active volcanoes, the question is not *if* it will erupt again (an
70 eruption is **inevitable**); the question is *when* it will happen.

"Every volcano works in a different way," explains Carlos Valdés González, a scientist who **monitors** El Popo. "What we're trying
75 to learn here are the symptoms signaling that

El Popo will erupt." These include earthquakes, or any sign that the mountain's surface is changing or **expanding**. The hope is that scientists will be able to warn people in the
80 surrounding areas so they have enough time to escape. A powerful eruption could **displace** over 20 million people—people whose lives can be saved if the warning is delivered early enough.

85 For many people living near El Popo— especially the farmers—**abandoning** their land is unthinkable. As anyone who farms near a volcano knows, the world's richest soils are volcanic. They produce bananas and coffee in
90 Central America, fine wines in California, and enormous amounts of rice in Indonesia.

Today, many people who live near El Popo continue to see the mountain as their **ancestors** did. According to ancient beliefs,
95 a volcano can be a god, a mountain, and a human all at the same time. To appease[3] El Popo and to ensure rain and a good harvest, locals begin a cycle of ceremonies that starts in March and ends in August. Carrying food
100 and gifts for the volcano, they hike up the mountain. Near the summit, they present their offerings, asking the volcano to protect and provide for one more season.

---

[3] If you **appease** someone, you try to stop them from being angry by giving them something they want.

Reading Comprehension

Multiple Choice. Choose the best answer for each question.

Main Idea

1. What is the third paragraph (starting line 18) mainly about?
   a. how Mount Fuji became an important religious site
   b. the healing properties of Mount Fuji
   c. reasons people climb Mount Fuji
   d. the visitors to Mount Fuji

Detail

2. Which of these statements about Mount Fuji is NOT true?
   a. It is the largest volcano in Japan.
   b. Scientists believe it may erupt soon.
   c. It has erupted recently.
   d. Locals have traditions concerning the mountain.

Vocabulary

3. In line 75, the word *symptoms* could be replaced with _____.
   a. earthquakes
   b. signs
   c. sounds
   d. lessons

Inference

4. Scientists can date the last great eruption of El Popo _____.
   a. by talking to people who experienced the event
   b. from videos of the eruption
   c. from investigating geological evidence
   d. from descriptions in religious books

Detail

5. What was the reason for the evacuation from El Popo in 2000?
   a. Ash and smoke were seen coming from the mountain.
   b. A large earthquake was felt.
   c. A change in the mountain's surface was noticed.
   d. A powerful eruption took place.

Detail

6. Which statement is true about both Mount Fuji and El Popo?
   a. They have both erupted recently.
   b. They are both less than 100 kilometers from a very large city.
   c. Locals present gifts to both volcanoes for protection.
   d. They both provide rich soil used for producing coffee.

Cohesion

7. The following sentence would best be placed at the end of which paragraph? *For this reason, people will stay on their land, even if they face danger.*
   a. 4 (starting line 31)
   b. 6 (starting line 55)
   c. 7 (starting line 72)
   d. 8 (starting line 85)

Critical Thinking

Inferring: Why do you think farmers would rather risk their lives than move and set up their farms away from a volcano?

_____

Discussion: Where do you think is the safest place in the world to live? Which is the most dangerous? Why?

Being an Active Reader

Active readers are fully engaged with a text, making connections and asking questions as they read. The following tips will help you be a more active reader.

1. Look at the title, headings, and photos. Use them to think about what you already know about the topic.
2. Circle any unfamiliar vocabulary. Write definitions in the text's margins.
3. Identify what each paragraph "says" (its main idea) and what it "does" (its purpose).
4. Connect ideas in the text. Notice words like *however*, *importantly*, and *finally*.
5. Write any questions you have about the text in the margin.
6. Make word webs, outlines, or charts to help you understand ideas visually.
7. Summarize the text in one or two sentences.
8. Create exam questions about the text. Share and discuss them with a partner.

A. Applying. Use the tips above as you read this text. Then discuss the questions (1–3) with a partner.

Living Near a Volcano

As world population grows, more people are living in dangerous areas, including near active volcanoes. The Decade Volcano Project has named 16 of these volcanoes as particularly worthy of investigation based on their potential for destruction.

The project aims to increase study of these particular volcanoes—their historical timeline for activity, how we can better predict future activity, and, most importantly, what people can do to prepare for an eruption.

It may seem strange to think of "defending" a town against a volcanic eruption, but the project already boasts several successes. For example, during the 1992 eruption of Mount Etna in Sicily, a lava flow was threatening the town of Zafferana. Local authorities blocked the flow in a tube that was feeding lava from higher up the slope. Flying in helicopters to keep a safe distance, they dropped large blocks of concrete into the tube's opening, successfully plugging it and diverting the lava away from the town.

1. Did you circle any vocabulary? Which words?
2. What is the main idea and purpose of each paragraph?
3. How would you summarize the text?

B. Discussion. With a partner, create three exam questions about the text. Share them with another pair.

∧ Italy's Mount Etna lights up the night sky.

Vocabulary Practice

A. Completion. Complete the information with words from the box. One word is extra.

> abandon   ancestors   dawn   disastrous   holy   monitor

Many legends (stories passed down from **1.** _____) involve volcanoes. According to *The Legend of Popo*, the two volcanoes of Popocatépetl and Iztaccíhuatl tell the story of a princess and a soldier named Popocatépetl, who fell in love, but with **2.** _____ consequences. In one version, Iztaccíhuatl dies of grief after she is told by her father that Popocatépetl has been killed in battle. When Popocatépetl returns from war to find her dead, he carries her body to the top of a nearby volcano. He refuses to **3.** _____ her body and he waits to die. Eventually, snow covers them both and they become two mountains.

It is said that the gods were touched by Popocatépetl's sacrifice of refusing to leave Iztaccíhuatl's body until he died. Today, smoke can often still be seen at **4.** _____ rising from the summit of the volcano, which many people regard as a mysterious and **5.** _____ place. According to legend, this is the torch of Popocatépetl, who still stands guard over his beloved's body.

B. Completion. Complete the paragraph with the correct form of words from the box.

> disaster   displace   expand   inevitable   monitor   witness

The islands of Hawaii rose out of the sea as a result of volcanic activity on the ocean floor. One of the islands' volcanoes, Mt. Kilauea, is currently the most active volcano on Earth, and Hawaiians have **1.** _____ its evolving shape over hundreds of years. Often, sections of earth are **2.** _____ by a sudden jolt, or pressure builds up under the surface as the hot molten rock **3.** _____, causing an eruption. Nowadays, the shape of the volcano is closely **4.** _____ by scientists. They know that a future eruption is **5.** _____, but they hope they can prevent it from being a **6.** _____ for the people who live nearby.

Word Link The prefix **ex-** can mean "away," "from," or "out," e.g., *expand, exceed, exit, explode, export.*

According to Hawaiian legend, Pele, the goddess of fire and volcanoes, lives in the top crater of Mt. Kilauea. The formations made by cooling lava were given names like Pele's Tears and Pele's Hair.

EARTHQUAKE ZONES

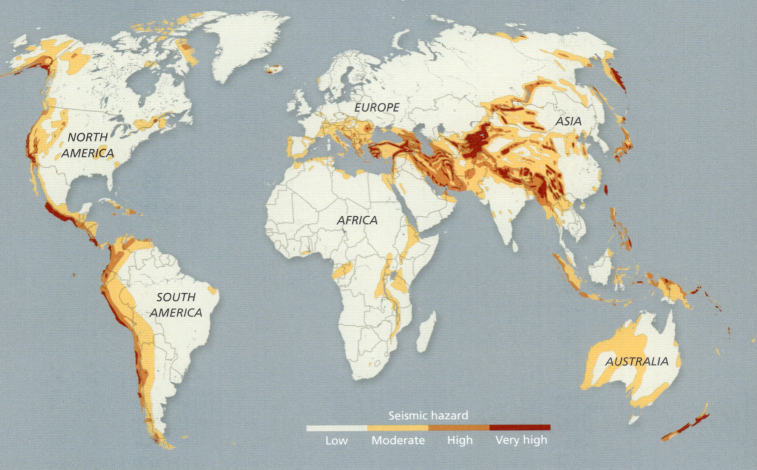

EUROPE

ASIA

NORTH
AMERICA

AFRICA

SOUTH
AMERICA

AUSTRALIA

Seismic hazard

Low   Moderate   High   Very high

Before You Read

A. True or False. The map above shows the areas that are most at risk of disastrous earthquakes. Read the sentences below (1–3), and circle **T** (True) or **F** (False).

1. Southern Europe and Central Asia have serious earthquakes.   **T**   **F**

2. People living along the east coasts of North and South America are often affected by earthquakes.   **T**   **F**

3. Australia has a low or moderate probability of earthquake.   **T**   **F**

B. Scan. Quickly scan the reading on pages 66–67 to answer this question: Does the author of this passage think that predicting earthquakes is possible? Then read the passage to check your answer.

The waves of an earthquake come > in two forms. P-waves (yellow) arrive fastest and compress and punch the rock. S-waves (red) are slower but more destructive. They move from side to side to shake and destroy buildings. The building features in blue, such as deep foundations, can protect a building from earthquakes.

Is Prediction Possible?

Never before have so many people packed into cities—places such as Los Angeles, Istanbul, Tokyo, and Lima—that are regularly affected by earthquakes. Located near the edge of Earth's huge, shifting plates, these cities face the risk of death and economic disaster from large quakes—and from the tsunamis, fires, and other destruction they often cause.

We understand earthquakes better than we did a century ago. Now, scientists would like to predict them, but is this possible? Today, some of the simplest questions about earthquakes are still difficult to answer: Why do they start? What makes them stop? Perhaps the most important question scientists need to answer is this: Are there clear patterns in earthquakes, or are they basically **random** and impossible to predict?

In Japan, government scientists say they have an answer to the question. "We believe that earthquake prediction is possible," says Koshun Yamaoka, a scientist at the Earthquake Research Institute at the University of Tokyo. Earthquakes follow a pattern; they have observable signs, Yamaoka believes. In fact, Japan has already predicted where its next great earthquake will be: Tokai, a region along the Pacific coast about 160 kilometers (100 miles) southwest of Tokyo. Here, two plate boundaries have generated huge earthquakes every 100 to 150 years. And it could be a **massive** quake. The section along Tokai hasn't had a major quake since 1854. The theory is that strain[1] is building up in this region, and that it's time for this **zone** to reduce its stress. Unfortunately, this is more a forecast

---

1 **Strain** is force or pressure that causes something to break or become damaged.

> "We believe that earthquake prediction is possible."
>
> Koshun Yamaoka, Research Scientist

than a prediction. It's one thing to say that an earthquake is likely to happen in a high-risk area. It's another to predict exactly where and when the quake will occur.

The desire for a **precise** prediction of time and place has led to another theory: the idea of "preslip." Naoyuki Kato, a scientist at the Earthquake Research Institute, says his **laboratory** experiments show that before a fault in the Earth's crust finally breaks and causes an earthquake, it slips[2] just a little. If we can **detect** these early slips taking place deep in the Earth's crust, we may be able to predict the next big quake.

Clues in the Desert

Scientists working in Parkfield, California, in the U.S. are also trying to see if predicting earthquakes is possible. They've chosen the town of Parkfield not only because the San Andreas Fault runs through it, but because it's known for having earthquakes quite regularly— approximately every 22 years. In the late 1980s, scientists in Parkfield decided to study the fault to see if there were any warning signs prior to a quake. To do this, they **drilled** deep into the fault and set up equipment to register activity. Then they waited for the quake.

Year after year, nothing happened. When a quake did finally hit on September 28, 2004, it was years off **schedule**, but most disappointing was the lack of warning signs. Scientists reviewed the data but could find no evidence of anything unusual preceding the September 28th quake. It led many to believe that perhaps earthquakes really are random events. Instead of giving up, though, scientists in Parkfield dug deeper into the ground. By late summer 2005, they had reached the fault's final depth of three kilometers (two miles), where they continued collecting **data**, hoping to find a clue.

And then they found something. In an article published in the July 2008 journal *Nature*, the researchers in Parkfield claimed to have detected small changes in the fault shortly before an earthquake hit. What had they noticed? Just before a quake, the cracks in the fault had widened slightly. Scientists registered the first changes ten hours before an earthquake of 3.0 on the Richter scale[3] hit; they identified identical signs two hours before a 1.0 quake—demonstrating that perhaps the "preslip" theory is correct. In other words, it may in fact be possible to predict an earthquake.

Although there is still a long way to go, it appears from the research being done all over the world that earthquakes are not entirely random. If this is so, in the future we may be able to **track** the Earth's movements and design early-warning systems that allow us to predict when a quake will happen and, in doing so, prevent the loss of life.

---

2 If something **slips**, it slides out of place.

3 The **Richter scale** is a scale used for measuring how severe an earthquake is. Higher numbers are more severe.

Reading Comprehension

Multiple Choice. Choose the best answer for each question.

Gist
1. What is the reading mainly about?
  a. earthquake prediction failures
  b. the Japanese government's work on earthquakes
  c. efforts to predict when an earthquake will happen
  d. the Parkfield investigations

Paraphrase
2. Which of the following is closest in meaning to the reading's first sentence, beginning *Never before have* . . . ?
  a. Many people who live in big cities have experienced earthquakes.
  b. Cities crowded with people are more likely to have serious earthquakes.
  c. Some of the biggest cities in the world suffer damage from earthquakes.
  d. More people than ever live in cities that are affected by earthquakes.

Reference
3. In line 61, what does *do this* refer to?
  a. wait for an earthquake
  b. study the fault
  c. predict an earthquake
  d. set up equipment

Vocabulary
4. In line 68, the word *reviewed* could be replaced with _____.
  a. recorded
  b. deleted
  c. saw
  d. studied

Detail
5. Which of the following statements is NOT true?
  a. A major earthquake occurs in Tokai every 100–150 years.
  b. Scientists believe that the "pre-slip" theory could help predict earthquakes.
  c. Data supporting the "pre-slip" theory was found in Parkfield.
  d. There was a major earthquake in Parkfield, in late summer 2005.

Cause and Effect
6. According to Parkfield scientists, how did cracks in the fault change before an earthquake hit?
  a. They became much wider.
  b. They became slightly narrower.
  c. They became slightly wider.
  d. They became much narrower.

Main Idea
7. What is the main idea of the last paragraph (starting line 90)?
  a. Further research will help us avoid loss of life in the future.
  b. Earthquake research has had a long and successful history.
  c. Early-warning systems are being designed to predict earthquakes.
  d. It is unlikely we will ever be able to predict the Earth's movement accurately.

Critical Thinking

Evaluating: In order to prove useful, how long before an earthquake should the early-warning system send a warning to the people?

_____

Discussion: Which type of natural disaster mentioned in this unit concerns you the most? Why?

Understanding Cause and Effect Relationships

> When writers explain a process, they often describe an action's cause and/or its effect. Words that indicate cause and effect relationships include *caused, as a result, because, so, therefore,* and *the reason*. As you read a text, try to make connections between events by asking questions that answer *What caused . . . ?* and *What was the result of . . . ?* an event.

A. Multiple Choice. Look back at the caption on page 66. Choose the correct answer for each question.

1. What is the main cause of buildings moving from side to side?
   a. P-waves
   b. S-waves

2. What effect can a building's deep foundations have?
   a. protect the building from earthquakes
   b. make a building more likely to be damaged by earthquakes

B. Completion. Read this text and answer the questions (1–2).

The San Francisco earthquake of 1906 left about 225,000 people homeless. However, more property was destroyed by fire than by the earthquake itself. Fires broke out in many parts of town after natural gas pipes broke. Other fires were accidentally started when firefighters, trying to create firebreaks, used explosives to destroy buildings. This resulted in the destruction of many buildings that might otherwise have survived the earthquake.

1. What two things caused fires to break out?

   _____

   _____ .

2. What did the use of firebreaks eventually lead to?

   _____

   _____ .

∧ A view looking down Pine Street in the wake of the 1906 earthquake, San Francisco, California, U.S.A.

Vocabulary Practice

A. Completion. Complete the sentences below using words from the box.

drill	massive	random	schedule	track	zone

1. Scientists _____ holes into the ground near earthquake fault areas to learn what is happening under the surface.

2. One reason earthquakes are so hard to predict is that they don't seem to follow any regular pattern or _____; they appear to occur almost at _____.

3. Scientists who _____ the movements of the Earth's crust believe that a _____ earthquake, known as "the Big One," will eventually occur in southern California.

4. Research after the 2004 Asian tsunami found only two dead buffaloes in a large wildlife conservation _____ in Sri Lanka. This led to renewed belief that animals are sensitive to the near arrival of earthquakes.

B. Completion. Complete the information with words from the box. One word is extra.

data	detect	laboratory	precise	schedule

Researchers collecting **1.** _____ from experiments in a **2.** _____, as well as those observing animals in the real world, suggest that animals are much more aware of the world around them than we human beings. For example, some scientists believe that dogs can be used to predict earthquakes. Mitsuaki Ota of Azabu University, Japan, claims that dogs can **3.** _____ big earthquakes about three hours before they happen. Some scientists are confident that with the help of dogs, one day more **4.** _____ predictions could be possible.

∧ A girl and her pet dog at a temporary shelter after the 1995 earthquake in Kobe, Japan. Researcher Mitsuaki Ota believes that some cats and dogs in the area were able to detect the quake before it happened.

Word Partnership
Use **schedule** with:
(*adj.*) **busy** schedule, **regular** schedule; (*n.*) **change of** schedule, **work** schedule, **train** schedule; (*prep.*) **according to** schedule, **ahead of** schedule, **behind** schedule, **on** schedule.

VIEWING Santorini Volcano

Before You Watch

A. Inferring. Read the caption below. What do you think scientists hope to learn from their research in Santorini?

∧ Scientists are investigating a volcano off the Greek island of Santorini. They believe a massive eruption in 1630 B.C. may have caused the Minoan civilization to vanish. The volcano is now mostly underwater.

While You Watch

A. Viewing. Check (✓) the topics that are mentioned in the video.

- ☐ a Minoan community called Akrotiri
- ☐ the eruption of the volcano Vesuvius
- ☐ why Robert Ballard and his team are studying Santorini's volcano
- ☐ why Ballard and his team were unable to reach Santorini's volcano
- ☐ an exciting underwater discovery near Santorini

B. Completion. Circle the words to complete each caption.

a. The volcano eruption (**completely buried / triggered the decline of**) the Akrotiri.

b. The scientists' goal was to see how big the (**last eruption was / next eruption will be**).

c. The scientists discovered the eruption was much (**smaller / larger**) than they had thought.

d. At the Kolumbo volcano, the scientists found (**a shipwreck / hot-water vents**).

After You Watch

A. Discussion. Discuss these questions with a partner.

1. Why were the scientists so excited to discover the hot-water vents?

2. What do you think Ballard means when he says that Santorini will "more than likely have a violent future"?

5

ISLANDS
AND BEACHES

The Two Brothers rock formations and Praia do Bode beach at sunset, Fernando de Noronha, Pernambuco, Brazil

Warm Up

Discuss these questions with a partner.

1. What makes a good place for a vacation?

2. Can you name any famous beaches? What do you know about them?

3. Why do you think islands are so popular with vacationers?

Before You Read

A. Quiz. Do you know where these beaches are? Match each beach to its location. Then check your answers on page 88.

1. _____ Ipanema Beach   **a.** the Philippines
2. _____ Waikiki Beach   **b.** Australia
3. _____ Bondi Beach   **c.** Brazil
4. _____ Maya Bay, Phi Phi Island   **d.** Thailand
5. _____ Boracay Beach   **e.** Florida, U.S.A.
6. _____ Miami Beach   **f.** Hawaii, U.S.A.

B. Skim. Look quickly at the title, first paragraph, photos, and captions in the passage on pages 75–77. Then answer these questions.

1. Who is Stanley Stewart, and what is he doing in Brazil?

2. What is your idea of "the perfect beach"? Read the passage to see if Stewart visits a place like the one you've described.

THE PERFECT BEACH

^ Prainha, Rio de Janeiro, Brazil

1   In **pursuit** of the perfect beach, travel writer Stanley Stewart heads to Brazil, where he discovers some of the world's most beautiful sandy escapes.

     I'm standing on Rio de Janeiro's Copacabana beach, one of
5   Brazil's—and the world's—most famous stretches[1] of sand. As I watch life go by here in all its varied forms, I've come to realize that any understanding of Brazil really begins on its beaches. In this vibrant, multicultural country, the beach is not just a place; it's a state of mind—a way of thinking and living.

10   Rio alone, I'm told, has over 70 beaches, each with its own community: Some are for bodybuilders, others are for senior citizens, still others are popular with parents and children. But Rio's beaches are just the starting point for my exploration of

---

1 A **stretch** of road, water, or land is a length of it.

Brazil's Atlantic coastline, which at more than 8,000 kilometers (5,000 miles), and with more than 2,000 beaches, is the longest in the world. Every Brazilian has his or her own ideas of the perfect beach and is **eager** to tell you where to find it. I'm happy to take people's advice, but my **ultimate** goal is to find my own dream beach.

I head to a place said to have some of Brazil's best coastline: the state of Bahia in the northeast. Portuguese settlers established themselves at Bahia's present-day capital, Salvador da Bahia, in 1549. Over the centuries, people of many races have arrived and intermarried here, creating a distinctive cultural mix, which influences Bahia's language, religion, cuisine, music, and dance.

I'd been told that one of Bahia's best beaches—Prainha—lies just south of Salvador, near the town of Itacaré. On arriving at Prainha's beach, I discover its golden sand lined by a row of perfect palm trees, moving softly in the ocean breeze. Under the moon, silver waves roll onto

Frigatebirds fly over a dramatic beach landscape in Fernando de Noronha, Brazil.

hangouts in the world (especially if you like windsurfing). It attracts visitors from Tokyo to Toronto and has grown from a small village into a lively little town. Despite the changes, Jeri hasn't been **spoiled** by tourists, mostly because of its **isolated** location—it's at least five hours from any airport.

Everyone in Jeri rents a beach buggy,[2] which comes with a driver. I tell my driver to take me as far along the coast as he can. We drive for three hours, finally arriving at Maceió, a fisherman's beach. Boats lie on their sides while nets hang out to dry on lines between fishermen's houses. We eat on the beach and later rest in hammocks near the table. It's a great day on an amazing beach. *How can it possibly get any better?* I wonder. But I have one final place to visit.

Of the many beach destinations in this country, there is one that all Brazilians hold in high regard—the islands of Fernando de Noronha. More than a dozen beautiful beaches ring the island of Fernando alone, three of which **rank** among the top ten in Brazil. The islands of Fernando de Noronha lie a few hundred kilometers out in the Atlantic. For years, people were **prohibited** from visiting these islands because they were used as a prison and later by the army. Today the islands are a national park and UNESCO World Heritage Site, rich with **diverse** bird and sea life.

I visit a number of beaches on Fernando, but I leave the best one for last. The beach at Praia do Leão is the perfect balance of sand, sea, and sky. The water is pale blue and warm, alive with colorful fish, turtles, and other marine[3] life; the sand is the color of honey. And in the rock formations and strong winds that occasionally come in from the Atlantic, there is that hint of wildness I was seeking. Finally, I've found the beach of my dreams. I dig my toes in the sand deeply and imagine I can hold on to this place forever.

the sand. As I enter the water, I have the feeling of swimming through moonlight. Prainha's beauty is **magnificent**—its perfect curves and graceful lines are like something you might see in a postcard. But for me, it's a little too perfect. The beach I'm searching for needs to be a little wilder . . .

I continue my search, heading north to one of Brazil's legendary beaches: Jericoacoara. Twenty years ago, only a handful of people were living in Jeri. Today it's an international **destination**, considered one of the best beach

---

2 A **beach buggy** is a small, open car with large wheels made for driving on a beach.

3 **Marine** is used to describe things related to the sea.

Reading Comprehension

Multiple Choice. Choose the best answer for each question.

Gist
1. What is the reading mainly about?
   a. Brazilian beach tourism
   b. an educational tour of South America's beaches
   c. the author's search for the dream beach
   d. little-known beaches of South America

Purpose
2. What is the purpose of paragraph 4 (starting line 22)?
   a. to describe Bahia's many beaches
   b. to explain why Bahia has the perfect beach
   c. to describe Bahia's music and dance scene
   d. to give information on Bahia's cultural background

Vocabulary
3. In line 45, the word *legendary* could be replaced
   with _____.
   a. oldest
   b. isolated
   c. picturesque
   d. famous

Inference
4. Which of these beaches is the most isolated?
   a. Copacabana
   b. Prainha
   c. Jericoacoara
   d. Maceió

Detail
5. The islands of Fernando de Noronha now _____.
   a. contain a prison
   b. are a national park
   c. are used by the army
   d. have many beach buggies

Reference
6. In line 81, *the best one* refers to _____.
   a. the collection of Fernando beaches
   b. Praia do Leão
   c. the pale blue water
   d. the marine life

Inference
7. Which type of beach would probably appeal to
   the author the most?
   a. busy, near a city, with lots of beach activities
   b. warm, isolated, a little wild, with rich animal life
   c. trendy, with a distinctive cultural mix
   d. crowded, with music and dance, blue water
      and palm trees

Critical Thinking

Inferring: Why do you think Stewart feels that Prainha is "a little too perfect"?

_____

Discussion: What do you think can be done to preserve beautiful beaches from the negative effects of the tourist trade?

Summarizing a Writer's Point of View

An author's point of view refers to his or her beliefs, opinions, and personal judgments toward a certain subject. In other words, it's how the author feels about what he or she is writing about. An author may have one strong and clear position, or may have conflicting views on the same issue. An author may clearly state how he or she feels, or leave it open to the reader's interpretation.

A. Matching. Below is a list of beaches that Stewart visited. Number the beaches **1–5** in the order he visited them. Then match each beach to Stewart's description. One description is extra.

☐ Praia do Leão •
☐ Copacabana •
☐ Maceió •
☐ Prainha •
☐ Jericoacoara •

• **a.** beautiful but too crowded
• **b.** the beach of my dreams
• **c.** remote village with beaches great for windsurfing
• **d.** great place to fish, eat, and relax
• **e.** one of the most famous beaches in the world
• **f.** picture perfect but not wild enough

B. Completion. Why does the author find Praia do Leão to be the perfect beach? Complete the information with words from the reading.

- on a cluster of islands that is a _____ park
- balance of _____, _____, and _____

- full of _____ life

The perfect beach:
Praia do Leão

- _____ from rock formations and wind

- _____ and pale blue water
- _____-colored sand

Vocabulary Practice

A. Completion. Complete the information with the correct words from the box. One word is extra.

destination	eager	isolated
prohibited	pursuit	ultimate

Writer seeks "wife" for a year on a tropical island.
How many women do you think would answer this ad?
A 24-year-old British woman named Lucy Irvine did. The
opportunity to survive in a(n) **1.** _____ place
provided her with the **2.** _____ challenge.

The ad was from a writer and adventurer named Gerald Kingsland.
As an adventurer herself, Irvine was **3.** _____
to try living on an empty tropical island. There were other
applicants in **4.** _____ of the job, but Irvine
eventually got it. And not long afterward, in May 1981, she was
heading for a(n) **5.** _____ on the other side
of the world . . .

B. Completion. Complete the information with the correct form
of words from the box.

diverse	magnificent	prohibit	rank	spoil

The uninhabited island Irvine and Kingsland were to live on was
Tuin, situated between Australia and Papua New Guinea. As
living there was **1.** _____ by law, they needed
Australia's permission, and were required to be legally married
in order to continue with their plan.

At first sight, the island looked like paradise, with white beaches
lined with palm trees, and clear blue water. However, their
experience was soon **2.** _____. This was
because getting access to a source of drinking water, which
3. _____ highest on their list of survival needs,
forced the pair to set up camp on a less attractive part of the island.
Also, their conflicting opinions on a(n) **4.** _____
range of subjects led to problems in their relationship. The
difficulties of working together proved too great, and despite
their **5.** _____ surroundings, the adventure
lasted only a year.

> **Word Partnership**
> Use **rank** with:
> (*adj.*) **high** rank, **top**
> rank; (*prep.*) rank
> **above**, rank **below**;
> (*adv.*) rank **high.**

LAND OF FIRE AND ICE

Before You Read

A. Matching. Read the caption and use the correct form of the words in **bold** to complete the definitions below.

1. A(n) _____ is a place that draws visitors because it is interesting or unusual.

2. A(n) _____ event has lots of interesting things happening in it.

3. Something that is _____ makes you admire it because it is great in size or done with great skill.

B. Scan. Scan for numbers on pages 82–83 to complete the following information about Iceland.

1. population: _____ people

2. area: _____ km²

3. age of language: _____ years

4. winter temperature: _____ degrees Celsius

5. daylight hours in summer: _____ hours

Iceland is famous for its **impressive** natural **attractions** such as Eldfell volcano and the "Blue Lagoon." Iceland also has a **lively** and exciting capital city, making it a great destination for tourists.

1 Never mind its chilly name—as a travel destination, Iceland is hot!

With the Atlantic Ocean to its south and the Greenland Sea to its north, Iceland is Europe's
5 westernmost country, with the world's most northerly capital city, Reykjavík. Viking explorers **migrated** to Iceland from northern Europe in 930 A.D., when they established the world's first parliament.[1] The country's national language
10 can still be traced to the one spoken by the Vikings over 1,000 years ago. Today, Iceland has a population of just over 310,000, spread over 100,000 square kilometers (about 40,000 square miles). Despite its small size, there are many
15 reasons to visit this remarkable country.

City of Culture

Most visitors' first port of call is Reykjavík, a small and clean city known for its colorful and stylish **architecture**. The city's downtown area is lined
20 with shops, art galleries, cafés, and bookstores. In 2000, Reykjavík was awarded the title of Europe's City of Culture, thanks to its art and museum scenes, and lively nightlife.

The good news for visitors is that Iceland's
25 temperatures are fairly mild, even in the winter when they stay at around four degrees Celsius (40° F). During winter months, nights are long, and the northern lights[2] become visible, lighting up the night sky with a **spectacular**
30 natural display.

In summer, the country gets almost 22 hours of daylight, and native Icelanders and visitors alike enjoy partying outdoors until dawn.

Hot Springs

35 Iceland is one of the most volcanically active nations in the world, and there are a number of thermal (hot water) springs around the island. All are heated **naturally** by underground volcanic activity. In fact, Iceland **converts** energy
40 generated by these springs into electricity, which powers and heats people's homes and businesses. As a result, Iceland burns very little fossil fuel, such as oil and gas, and has some of the cleanest air in the world.

45 One of Iceland's most popular hot springs is the Blue Lagoon, a huge lake of bright blue seawater just outside Reykjavík. Surrounded by volcanoes and lava fields, the Blue Lagoon receives more than 300,000 visitors a year.
50 After a long day's sightseeing or a long night of partying, visitors can relax their muscles and release their **tension** in the lagoon's steaming hot water, which has an average temperature of about 38 degrees (100° F). Some believe the
55 waters are able to **cure** certain illnesses and improve skin quality.

Caves and Monsters

Most of the inner part of Iceland is uninhabited[3] and accessible only by truck or other **vehicle**.
60 Nevertheless, there is a range of outdoor activities to enjoy elsewhere in the country, particularly along the coasts: "Iceland is an adventure," said Sol Squire, whose Icelandic company organizes adventure trips around the
65 country. "We have Europe's biggest glaciers, active volcanoes, cave explorations, and skiing."

One of Iceland's most popular attractions is caving. Exploring Iceland's unusual lava caves, most of which formed more than 10,000 years
70 ago, requires only basic caving knowledge and equipment. Ice caves, however, are more challenging and require special clothes and hiking tools. The best-known ice caves are in Vatnajökull—a layer of ice which, at 8,000
75 square kilometers (3,000 square miles), is Iceland's—and Europe's—largest glacier. It also happens to be situated just above an active volcano!

---

1 A **parliament** of a country is the group of elected people who make or change laws.

2 **The northern lights** (also called the "aurora borealis") are colored lights often seen in the night sky in places near the Arctic Circle.

3 If a place is **uninhabited**, no one lives there.

A lonely house stands on the shore of Hrisey Island.

If exploring caves and glaciers doesn't interest you, head south, just outside the town of Vík, to check out[4] the huge rock formations that were once believed to be **monsters** turned into stone. These are a dramatic part of the scenery on one of Iceland's most magnificent black-sand beaches.

The Golden Circle

And finally, no trip to Iceland would be complete without a visit to the Golden Circle, a pathway northeast of Reykjavík that connects Gullfoss (a huge "Golden Waterfall"), the hot springs region of Geysir, and Thingvellir National Park. The mid-Atlantic fault that runs through Iceland is **literally** pulling the island apart. Nowhere is this more evident than in the Thingvellir Valley, where the land is actually separating and the stony ground beneath your feet frequently shifts. Hold on while you hike!

---

4 If you **check out** something, you look at it or try to find out more about it.

Reading Comprehension

Multiple Choice. Choose the best answer for each question.

Paraphrase

1. Which of the following is closest in meaning to:
   *Despite its small size, there are many reasons to visit
   this remarkable country* (lines 14–15)?
   a. There are many reasons this country is considered
      to be too small to visit.
   b. There are a lot of attractions in this interesting country,
      even though it is so small.
   c. This is an unusual country to visit because it is so small.
   d. Small countries are usually perceived as boring,
      but Iceland is different.

Inference

2. Which is the best place to go if you like to party?
   a. Vatnajökull
   b. Reykjavík
   c. the Blue Lagoon
   d. Thingvellir Valley

Detail

3. What are the hot springs of the Blue Lagoon heated by?
   a. solar energy
   b. volcanic activity
   c. electrical power
   d. fossil fuels

Vocabulary

4. In line 94, the word *evident* could be replaced with _____.
   a. dangerously separated
   b. strangely beautiful
   c. quietly formed
   d. easily seen

Detail

5. What is the Golden Circle?
   a. the most popular area to visit in Reykjavík's city center
   b. a scenic walk around the Blue Lagoon
   c. a pathway that connects a park, a waterfall, and hot springs
   d. a road that goes around the coast of Iceland

Detail

6. Where is the mid-Atlantic fault most noticeable?
   a. Reykjavík
   b. the Blue Lagoon
   c. Thingvellir Valley
   d. Geysir

Inference

7. Who is this passage probably written for?
   a. tourists
   b. scientists
   c. business travelers
   d. Icelanders

Critical Thinking

Evaluating: Do you think the author gives an unbiased view of Iceland? Why or why not?

_____

Discussion: What type or types of tourists do you think Iceland would appeal to? Why?

Labeling Details on a Map

Some texts may include maps, illustrations, diagrams, or other visuals. These can help you better understand a text by allowing you to see information in a more visual way. As you read a text, try to make connections between the text and the visual(s). It can be helpful to label or add details to the visual(s) with information from the text.

A. Labeling. Look back at the first paragraph (starting line 3) of the reading on page 82–83. Use the information to complete the three missing labels on the map (1–3).

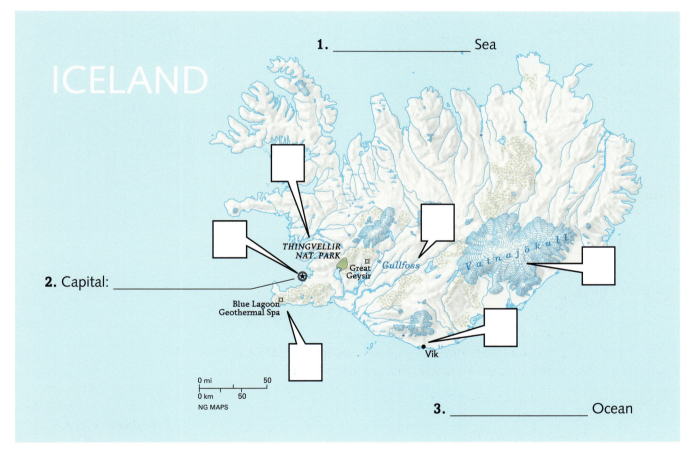

1. _____ Sea

ICELAND

THINGVELLIR NAT. PARK

Great Geysir   Gullfoss

Vatnajökull

2. Capital: _____

Blue Lagoon Geothermal Spa

Vík

0 mi   50
0 km   50
NG MAPS

3. _____ Ocean

B. Labeling. Label the map above with the activity from the list below (**a–f**) that visitors can do at each location.

   a. go caving
   b. view the mid-Atlantic fault
   c. see a large waterfall
   d. look at art
   e. visit huge rock formations near a black-sand beach
   f. relax in steaming hot water

Vocabulary Practice

A. Completion. Complete the information with the correct form of words from the box. Two words are extra.

architecture	convert	cure	migrate
literally	spectacular	tension	vehicle

1. Taroko Gorge on the island of Taiwan is a(n) _____ natural attraction.

2. The Taj Mahal is one of the world's great achievements of _____.

3. The beaches of Bali are a great destination for relieving your _____.

4. Some governments want to ban _____ from historic areas of their cities.

5. The mosque of Córdoba, Spain, was _____ to a church in the thirteenth century.

6. Peru's World Heritage Site Machu Picchu _____ means "Old Mountain."

B. Definitions. Read the information below. Then complete the definitions using the correct form of the words in **red**.

1. Most caves are formed **naturally** by the long, slow weathering of rocks.

2. Some scientists think it's possible that some plants in the rainforests of Madagascar could contain **cures** for diseases like cancer.

3. A strange creature with flippers and a beaklike mouth, now referred to as the "Montauk **monster**," washed up on a New York beach in 2008.

4. The island nation of Singapore was built by the hard work of people who **migrated** there from other countries.

   a. things that restore health _____

   b. a beastlike animal _____

   c. without artificial aid _____

   d. to move to a new or different country _____

∧ Taroko National Park is one of the world's natural wonders

Thesaurus
spectacular
Also look up:
(*adj.*) *impressive, stunning, incredible, breathtaking, sensational*

VIEWING | Pacific Paradise

Before You Watch

A. Definition. Read the information and then circle the correct definition for each word.

∧ Coral is clearly visible under the surface of an atoll's tropical lagoon in Ahe, in French Polynesia.

The **tropical** islands of French Polynesia in the South Pacific are **paradise** to many people. However, the tiny **atolls** are under threat. Rising seas caused by global warming may mean that these beautiful islands will disappear someday.

1. tropical
   a. relating to an area with tourists   b. relating to the warm area near the equator

2. paradise
   a. the place where you were born   b. a place that seems perfect

3. atoll
   a. a small group of low, coral islands   b. group of high, mountainous islands

B. Discussion. Discuss these questions with a partner.
   1. What do you think are some of the pros and cons of living on a tropical island?
   2. What are some ways people on islands can earn money?

While You Watch

A. Noticing. Check (✓) the ways of earning income in the Tuamotus that are discussed in the video.

a. ☐ fishing

b. ☐ tourism

c. ☐ copra

d. ☐ black pearls

B. Summarize. Complete the summary of the video using the correct form of words from the box. One word is extra.

diversity	eager	isolate	pursuit	ultimate	vast

The small, **1.** _____ islands of the Tuamotus are hidden among the waters of the **2.** _____ Pacific Ocean. The islands have mild tropical weather and are filled with a rich **3.** _____ of sea life.

As global warming causes sea levels to rise, these tiny but magnificent islands will become smaller, and may one day disappear. Many vacationers come here in **4.** _____ of a taste of paradise. They are **5.** _____ to experience the islands' sights, before they are gone forever.

After You Watch

A. Discussion. Discuss these questions with a partner.

1. Look back at your answers for question 1 of part **B** on page 87. Have your ideas changed after watching the video?

2. What place would you describe as "paradise"? Why?

Answers to Before You Read, page 74:
1. c; **2.** f; **3.** b; **4.** d; **5.** a; **6.** e

6

SUCCESS
AND FAILURE

A young girl rock climbing in Flagstaff, Arizona, U.S.A.

Warm Up

Discuss these questions with a partner.

1. Can you think of people who have achieved success despite great challenges or dangers?

2. Why do you think those people were successful?

3. Do you think failure can be a positive thing?

Before You Read

A. Quiz. How much of a risk-taker[1] are you? Circle your answers to the questions below, and then add up your numbers. The higher your score, the more of a risk-taker you are. Who are the biggest risk-takers in your class?

Would you . . .	No way.	Maybe.	Yes, probably.
go skydiving with a friend?	1	2	3
drive a car fast for fun?	1	2	3
go to a club alone?	1	2	3
sing, dance, or act in a school talent show?	1	2	3
live in a foreign country for a year on your own?	1	2	3
start your own company?	1	2	3
		My total score:	_____

1 A **risk-taker** is a person who likes adventure and isn't afraid of things that are new, challenging, or even dangerous. If you **take risks**, you do something even though the result might be negative.

B. Predict. Why do you think some people are bigger risk-takers than others? Make a list of your ideas. Then read the passage closely to check your ideas.

THE NATURE OF RISK

1   A diver descends into an underwater cave, a scientist researches a dangerous disease, and an entrepreneur[1] invests in a new business.

Each time we try something new, we take a risk. Sometimes, like
5 the diver or the businessman, we take big risks, usually for obvious reasons—for fame, for money, or to save lives. Most people will take some risk to achieve one of these goals. But as the danger increases, the number of people **willing** to go forward decreases. Only extreme risk-takers continue on. The question is: What
10 exactly **drives** these people to go on when others would stop?

---

1 An **entrepreneur** is a person who starts his or her own business.

Timothy Treadwell (above left) spent 13 summers photographing grizzly bears in Alaska. In 2003, Treadwell and his girlfriend were killed by one of the bears they were studying.

The Biology of Risk

To answer this question, scientists are studying the **biological** factors involved in risk-taking. Their research focuses on
15 certain chemicals in the brain. An important chemical in risk-taking is dopamine. It motivates us to seek out and learn new things, and it helps us process emotions like **anxiety** and fear. People whose
20 brains don't produce enough dopamine often lack motivation and interest in life. On the other hand, "someone who takes risks to accomplish something—to climb a mountain or start a company—that's
25 driven by motivation, and motivation is driven by dopamine," says Larry Zweifel, a neurobiologist at the University of Washington. "It's what **compels** humans to move forward."

30 When we accomplish a task, dopamine produces a feeling of **satisfaction**; it makes us feel good. The riskier the task, the more dopamine we produce, and the better we feel. Given this, why isn't everyone trying
35 to climb mountains or start businesses? In part, it's because of small molecules[2] called autoreceptors. These receptors control dopamine use in the brain. A person with more autoreceptors tends to be more careful,
40 as there is less dopamine moving freely around his or her brain. "Think of dopamine like gasoline," says neuropsychologist David Zald. The autoreceptors, on the other hand, are like the brakes on a car. A person who is
45 less able to use brakes is more likely to take risks.

Dealing with Fear

Dopamine production may make us feel good, but being in a high-risk situation for
50 an extended period of time is also stressful and can be dangerous. Successful risk-takers must learn to deal with the fear **associated**

A diver has a close encounter with a southern right whale in waters off the Auckland Islands, New Zealand.

with high-risk situations to reduce stress and stay safe.

55 In reality, **adapting** to risk is something we all learn to do. Take, for example, learning to drive a car. At first, a new driver may be afraid to travel on freeways. In time, though, as the driver gains experience, he or she will move comfortably into
60 speeding traffic and will worry less about the danger. Similarly, a tightrope walker first learns to walk on a beam on the ground. Later, he or she

---

2 A **molecule** is a very small chemical substance.

moves to a rope just off the ground, and then finally to the high wire. By this point, the tightrope walker is in control and the activity doesn't feel dangerous. By practicing a challenging activity, humans can become used to the risk, **manage** the danger, and control the fear that they feel in those situations.

The work that marine biologist and deep-sea diver Rhian Waller does illustrates this well. She studies life in some of the deepest and coldest waters on Earth. How does Waller control her fear and stay safe in these high-risk situations?

"It comes with practice," she says. "It's knowing exactly what to do when something goes wrong. We prepare well for each of our expeditions, and we try to **minimize** the number of risks we take."

Of course, a person doesn't have to be a tightrope walker or a deep-sea diver to be a risk-taker. Taking risks is part of being human. We are all motivated to experience new things. In order to do so, we have to take chances and, of course, we may fail.

Reading Comprehension

Multiple Choice. Choose the best answer for each question.

Cause and Effect

1. According to the article, what is a common reason for people to take large risks?
   a. a desire for fame
   b. a lack of dopamine
   c. to control motivation
   d. to learn new things

Detail

2. What is one of the main functions of dopamine?
   a. It allows us to talk.
   b. It allows us to be alert.
   c. It helps us process emotions.
   d. It makes us fear dangerous situations.

Vocabulary

3. The word *just* (line 63) could be replaced with _____.
   a. slightly   b. only
   c. recently   d. finally

Detail

4. What do autoreceptors do?
   a. They make us less careful.
   b. They make us feel better.
   c. They control dopamine in our brain.
   d. They connect molecules in our brain.

Cohesion

5. The following sentence would best be placed at the end of which paragraph? *But with enough practice, we might also succeed.*
   a. 2 (starting line 12)   b. 4 (starting line 48)
   c. 5 (starting line 55)   d. 7 (starting line 80)

Purpose

6. What is the purpose of paragraph 5 (starting line 55)?
   a. to show why driving and tightrope walking are such risky activities
   b. to give examples of how practicing a risky activity can reduce fear of it
   c. to illustrate how some people are attracted to risky activities while others aren't
   d. to explain why some activities are riskier and more dangerous than others

Inference

7. What can we infer about marine biologist Rhian Waller?
   a. She has learned to adapt to risk.
   b. She has been afraid of the ocean for most of her life.
   c. She prefers to do her job when there is danger involved.
   d. She thinks it is impossible to prepare for most risks.

Critical Thinking

Relating: The author claims that by practicing a challenging activity over and over again, we can control our fear of it. Can you think of an example of when you did this?

_____

Discussion: What advice would you give someone who took a risk, and failed?

Recognizing Metaphors

Writers use metaphors as a way to make a comparison. In a metaphor, a writer says that one thing is another thing in order to show or suggest that they are similar. Metaphors are a common part of language that add to the richness of a text. They can be found in many contexts, from literature to advertising to scientific texts. Below are a few examples.

I'm an early bird.   *Her home is a prison.*

She has a heart of gold.   *The homework was a breeze.*

A. Matching. Match the words to create common metaphors. Can you guess their meanings?

1. Time is _____.   **a.** blind
2. Love is _____.   **b.** a journey
3. Life is _____.   **c.** money
4. Blood is _____.   **d.** golden
5. Silence is _____.   **e.** an island
6. No man is _____.   **f.** thicker than water

B. Multiple Choice. Choose the correct answer to complete each sentence.

1. *Their father is a rock.* This means that their father is _____.

   a. old and stubborn   b. strong and reliable

2. *Her answer was music to his ears.* This means that her answer _____.

   a. made him very happy   b. sounded very pretty

3. *He's a sheep.* This means he's a _____.

   a. leader, not a follower   b. follower, not a leader

C. Identifying Metaphors. Look back at paragraph 3 (starting line 30) on page 92. What parts of a car does the author compare autoreceptors and dopamine to? Why does the author use these metaphors?

A. Completion. Complete the information by circling the correct word or phrase in each pair.

Herpetologists are **1. (compelling / willing)** to go to the far corners of the Earth in search of snakes. Snakes are not usually **2. (driven by / associated with)** saving lives, but their venom[1] is collected to see if any can be turned into lifesaving drugs. It's risky work, and a herpetologist has to **3. (minimize / compel)** the dangers of being around deadly snakes.

Herpetologists find it worth the risk because it would give them great **4. (management / satisfaction)** to find a toxin for medicinal use. There are 100,000 different venomous snakes species. The number of potential medications that could be found—and the number of people whose lives could be saved—is what **5. (compels / adapts)** these researchers to take such risks.

_____

1 A snake's **venom** is the poison it puts into your body when it bites you.

B. Completion. Complete the sentences using the correct form of words from the box.

adapt	associated with	compel
anxiety	biological	manage

1. Two things that are _____ each other are connected in some way.
2. _____ is used to describe the natural processes that occur in living things.
3. A person experiencing _____ feels nervous or worried.
4. If somebody _____ you to do something, they force you to do it.
5. When you _____ to a new situation, you change your ideas or behavior to deal with it successfully.
6. When you _____ something, you are in charge of running it or controlling it.

∧ Herpetologists risk their lives in the search for lifesaving venom.

Word Link The word root **min-** means "lesser" or "smaller," e.g., _minimize, minimal, minimum, minus, minority_.

THE REWARDS OF FAILURE

Before You Read

A. Discussion. Look at the photo and read the caption. Then discuss the questions with a partner.

1. Was Ernest Shackleton's expedition to Antarctica a success or a failure? Why?

2. Can you think of any famous failures? What happened? Why were they not successful?

B. Predict. What are some important things we can learn from failure? Make a list with a partner. As you read, check your ideas.

In 1914, British explorer Ernest Shackleton led an expedition to Antarctica, hoping to be the first person to cross the continent. Within months, his ship, the *Endurance* (above), became trapped in ice. Shackleton's goal changed from the completion of his expedition to the survival of his crew. In the end, he managed to lead all 27 of his men to safety.

Gerlinde Kaltenbrunner and other expedition members climb a slope toward K2's Camp II. ❯

1 Failure: We all avoid it, and most of us fear it. However, without failure, progress would be impossible. Indeed, the word *success* comes

5 from the Latin *succedere*, meaning "to come after." And what does success usually come after? Failure. It seems that one cannot exist without the other.

10 Learning from Failure

Every failure—even the worst ones—helps us learn to do things differently in the future. "I learned how *not* to climb the first four times

I tried to summit[1] Everest," says mountaineer Pete

15 Athans, who has now reached the world's highest peak seven times. "Failure gives you a chance to **refine** your approach. You're taking risks more and more intelligently." In Athans' case, his setbacks[2]

20 taught him that it was important to choose a less challenging route for his first climb up Everest. Learning from past mistakes and making changes helped him to reach the top successfully.

Failure also **reminds** us that things can go wrong—sometimes with disastrous results.

25 Austrian Gerlinde Kaltenbrunner is the first woman to summit all 14 of the world's 8,000-meter peaks without extra oxygen. In 2007, while climbing in Nepal, she was in an avalanche.[3] Luckily, she

---

1 If you **summit** a mountain, you reach the top.
2 A **setback** is something that happens that slows or stops progress.
3 An **avalanche** is a large amount of snow that falls down a mountain.

> # "...I couldn't stop climbing—this is my life."
> ### Gerlinde Kaltenbrunner

survived, but two nearby Spanish climbers died. The experience taught Kaltenbrunner that no matter how prepared a person is, bad things can still happen. The events of that day troubled her deeply, but in time, Kaltenbrunner decided she had to learn from the experience and **move on**. "I realized that I couldn't make the tragedy unhappen," she says, "and I couldn't stop climbing—this is my life."

The Value of Negative Results

Accepting failure is not easy for many, though. We are often **reluctant** to admit failure because our professional **reputations** depend on success. However, things are slowly changing, notably in the fields of business and science. In the past decade, for instance, some scientific journals—mostly in medicine and conservation—have published reports of failed experiments. The belief is that the science **community** can also learn from "negative" results and that this can eventually lead to positive **outcomes**.

In many ways, the business world already understands the value of negative results. To encourage entrepreneurship, the Netherlands-based ABN AMRO bank started an Institute of Brilliant Failures to learn more about what works and what doesn't in banking. Similarly, Eli Lilly and Company, the pharmaceutical corporation, has "R&D[4] outcome celebrations"—failure parties—to study data about drugs that don't work. (Almost 90 percent of all drug trials fail, and the drugs cannot be sold.)

In fact, one of the business world's most famous failures eventually became one of its biggest successes, in part because the product's makers learned from their mistakes. In the early 1990s, Apple Corporation created a handheld device called the Apple Newton. The product, though unique at the time, was expensive and heavy; moreover, some of its most important features didn't work properly. **Consequently**, it became one of Apple's biggest failures, and in 1998, the company stopped selling it. However, Apple's CEO, Steve Jobs, believed the product had potential and he began to explore ways of improving it. **In time**, this led to the creation of the iPhone and the iPad, two of the company's most successful products.

The story of the Apple Newton can teach us another important lesson about failure. Not only should we try to learn from it; if we want to succeed, we must also be **persistent**. Though Apple stopped selling the Newton in 1998, the first iPhone wasn't available until 2007. It took a lot of research and hard work to go from the Apple Newton to iPhone, but in the end, the effort paid off.[5]

Ultimately, there is a lot we can learn by studying mistakes. Perhaps the most important lesson is that failure and success are two sides of the same coin. One truly cannot exist without the other.

---

4 **R&D** is an abbreviation for *Research and Development*.
5 If something **pays off**, it is successful.

Reading Comprehension

Multiple Choice. Choose the best answer for each question.

Gist
1. What is the best way to summarize the reading passage?
   a. Success and fear are basically the same thing.
   b. Failure is always followed by success.
   c. You may need to fail before you can succeed.
   d. Accepting failure is very difficult.

Purpose
2. What is the purpose of the second and third paragraphs?
   a. to teach us what not to do when mountain climbing
   b. to convince us that success is something anyone can achieve
   c. to show how bad things can happen in any situation
   d. to give examples of how failure can be a good thing

Detail
3. Why are some scientific journals starting to publish the results of failed experiments?
   a. to encourage new experiments in other fields
   b. so that people can discuss and share their findings at failure parties
   c. to admit that the scientific community makes mistakes
   d. because of the belief that negative results can lead to successful outcomes

Detail
4. Which of the following is NOT true about the Apple Newton?
   a. It was heavy and expensive.
   b. Some of its features didn't work properly.
   c. It was a unique handheld device.
   d. It was Apple's first successful product.

The Apple Newton

Cause and Effect
5. According to the passage, what did the experience of the Apple Newton eventually lead to?
   a. Steve Jobs becoming Apple's CEO
   b. the creation of the iPad and iPhone
   c. a move toward selling more expensive products
   d. the introduction of a cheaper version of the product

Vocabulary
6. In line 86, the word *Ultimately* could be replaced by _____.
   a. Finally
   b. However
   c. After that
   d. For example

Inference
7. Which advice would the author most likely agree with?
   a. If you want to be successful, ask successful people what they did to succeed.
   b. Accept that some people fail and not everyone is meant to succeed.
   c. If you make a mistake, ask yourself what went wrong and try to learn from it.
   d. You should think of failure and success as the same thing.

Critical Thinking

Inferring: The reading says that *failure and success are two sides of the same coin.* What do you think this metaphor means?

_____

Discussion: What is something you have been successful at? Did you fail at it first?

Understanding Transitions

Transitions are words and phrases used to connect one idea to the next. They help texts flow more smoothly. Transitions have different purposes. Look at the following sentences and the various types of transitions they contain.

She was prepared for the trip. *However*, her partner was not. (contrast)

She was prepared for the trip. *As a result*, it was a great success. (consequence)

She was prepared for the trip. *In fact*, she was the most prepared of all. (emphasis)

A. Classification. Complete the chart with the correct transitions from the box.

above all	in short	likewise	moreover	therefore	yet

Adding	Contrasting	Similarity
additionally	however	similarly
in addition	nonetheless	in the same way
_____	_____	_____

Emphasizing	Consequence	Concluding
in fact	as a result	to conclude
indeed	consequently	ultimately
_____	_____	_____

B. Analyzing. Circle the correct transition in each sentence in 1–4. Then check your answers in the reading on pages 98–99.

1. Failure: We all avoid it, and most of us fear it. **However / In fact**, without failure, progress would be impossible. (lines 1–3)

2. . . . bank started an Institute of Brilliant Failures to learn more about what works and what doesn't in banking. **Above all, / Similarly,** Eli Lilly and Company, the pharmaceutical corporation, has failure parties to study data about drugs that don't work. (lines 48–59)

3. The product, though unique at the time, was expensive and heavy; **moreover, / nonetheless,** some of its most important features didn't work properly. (lines 66–69)

4. . . . some of its most important features didn't work properly. **To conclude, / Consequently,** it became one of Apple's biggest failures . . . (lines 68–70)

Vocabulary Practice

A. Completion. Complete the information below with the correct word in each pair.

When he was young, Beethoven had difficulty handling the violin. He also preferred to play his own music rather than **1. (refine / move on)** his technique. **2. (Consequently / Community)**, his teacher called him hopeless. Beethoven was **3. (persistent / reluctant)**, however. Today, he has a(n) **4. (reputation / outcome)** for being one of the greatest composers of all time.

Similarly, the famous dancer Fred Astaire experienced failure before success. Early in his movie career, Astaire received a note from a studio saying "Can't sing. Can't act. Can dance a little." He kept that note to **5. (remind / refine)** himself to never give up. **6. (In time / Reluctantly)**, he became one of the most successful dancers of the 20th century.

▽ Dancer Fred Astaire refused to let early criticism affect his dream of becoming a movie star.

B. Definitions. Complete the definitions using the correct form of words from **A**.

1. If you _____, you finish one activity and start doing something different.

2. A(n) _____ is all of the people who live in a particular area or place.

3. A person who is _____ is determined and does not give up easily.

4. To _____ something means to improve it by making small changes to it.

5. If you are _____ to do something, you are not eager to do.

6. A(n) _____ is a final product or an end result.

> **Word Partnership** Use **reputation** with: (*adj.*) **excellent** reputation, **well-deserved** reputation, **bad** reputation; (*n.*) reputation **for excellence**, reputation **for reliability**, reputation **for quality**.

VIEWING Savage Mountain

A. Discussion. Look at this information about the two highest mountains in the world. Then discuss the questions below with a partner.

1. Which mountain is higher?
2. Which mountain is more difficult to climb?
3. Which mountain is more popular with climbers? Why do you think so?
4. K2 is known as "the savage mountain." What do you think *savage* means?

MOUNT EVEREST

Location: **Nepal**
Elevation: **8,848 meters (29,035 feet)**
First climbed: **1953**
Expedition length: **65 days**
Technical difficulty: **4 out of 5**
Number to reach summit: **more than 5,600**
Death rate: **5.7%**

K2

Location: **Pakistan**
Elevation: **8,611 meters (28,251 feet)**
First climbed: **1954**
Expedition length: **75 days**
Technical difficulty: **5 out of 5**
Number to reach summit: **more than 300**
Death rate: **23.2%**

A. True or False. Mark the statements **T** (True) or **F** (False).

1. Heidi Howkins has climbed mountains on four continents. T F
2. Pakistan means "land of the savage mountain." T F
3. K2 is steeper and more remote than Mount Everest. T F
4. Over 500 people have died climbing K2. T F
5. Heidi was able to reach K2's summit. T F

B. Completion. Read what Heidi says about her life as a mountain climber. Complete the sentences using words from the box. Two words are extra.

afraid best die lucky personality snow step swimming

"Just before I left, literally the last words she said to me were, 'Please don't

1. _____.' Finally, I recovered enough to say, 'I'll do my

2. _____ to come back.'"

"It's a really ominous, forbidding mountain. It's got a character, a

3. _____ about it. And I don't think you can conquer it. I think you can . . . you can get 4. _____."

"You have to be so focused. You have to be mentally capable of driving yourself to take that extra 5. _____, when stopping [and] sitting down in the

6. _____ means dying."

After You Watch

A. Discussion. Discuss these questions with a partner.

1. In what ways could you consider Heidi's attempt a success?
2. What do you think Heidi learned from her attempt at reaching the summit?

7

GLOBAL ADDICTIONS

A huge traffic jam causes congestion on a street in Bangkok, Thailand.

Warm Up

Discuss these questions with a partner.

1. If you are addicted to something, you cannot stop consuming it. What things can people become addicted to?

2. Is it OK to be addicted to certain things? If so, what kinds of things?

3. Some people say that humans are addicted to fossil fuels like coal and oil. Do you agree?

Before You Read

A. Matching. Look at the information below. How many milligrams (mg) of caffeine do you think is in each item? Match a letter from the chart (**a**–**h**) to each item. Then check your answers on page 120.

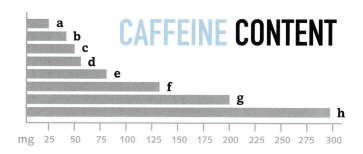

CAFFEINE CONTENT

Caffeine is a naturally occurring substance that can affect a person's nervous system. Most people associate caffeine with coffee, but it can also be found in many other familiar items.

1. Espresso coffee, 30 ml (1 oz) _____
2. Milk chocolate bar, 170 g (6 oz) _____
3. Brewed tea, 240 ml (8 oz) cup _____
4. Can of energy drink, 240 ml (8 oz) _____
5. Brewed coffee, 360 ml (12 oz) cup _____
6. Bottle of cola, 600 ml (20 oz) _____
7. Large soda drink, 1.7 l (64 oz) _____
8. Pain relief medicine (2 tablets) _____

B. Discussion. Do you think caffeine is good for you? Read the passage on pages 107–108 to check your ideas.

CAFFEINE:
THE WORLD'S FAVORITE DRUG

1   **It's 1:45 a.m.,** and 21-year-old Thomas Murphy is burning the midnight oil,[1] studying for an important engineering exam he has at 2:00 in the afternoon later today. To stay awake and focused, he's had two cups
5   of coffee in the last three hours and is now downing a popular energy drink—one that has two to three times the amount of caffeine as a similar sized can of soda. Many students like Murphy, as well as marathon runners, airline pilots, and long-distance travelers, owe
10   their energy—and sometimes their efficiency—to one of humankind's oldest stimulants:[2] caffeine.

     The power to counter[3] physical fatigue[4] and increase alertness is part of the reason caffeine ranks as the world's most popular mood-altering[5] drug. It is found
15   not only in sodas, energy drinks, coffee, and tea, but also in diet pills, pain relievers (like aspirin), and chocolate bars. Many societies around the world have also created entire **rituals** around the use of caffeine: afternoon tea in the U.K., the café culture of France, the tea ceremony
20   in Japan, and the morning cup of coffee or tea that in many cultures marks the start of the day.

     Caffeine is present in many of the foods or drinks we consume, but is it really good for us? Charles Czeisler, a scientist and sleep expert at Harvard Medical School,
25   believes that caffeine causes us to lose sleep, which he says is unhealthy. "Without adequate sleep—the typical eight hours—the human body will not function at its best, physically, mentally, or emotionally." Too often, Czeisler says, we consume caffeine to stay awake, which
30   later makes it impossible for us to get the rest we need.

∧ Ripening berries on the stem of a coffee plant

---

1 If someone is **burning the midnight oil**, they are staying up very late in order to study or do some other work.

2 A **stimulant** is a substance that can temporarily increase the activity of body processes.

3 To **counter** something is to produce an effect that is opposite of what is being experienced.

4 **Fatigue** is the feeling of extreme mental or physical tiredness.

5 A **mood-altering** substance is capable of causing changes in your mood.

Health risks have also been tied to caffeine consumption. Over the years, studies have attributed higher rates of certain types of cancer and bone disease to caffeine consumption. To date, however, there is no proof that caffeine actually causes these diseases.

A number of scientists, including Roland Griffiths, a professor at the Johns Hopkins School of Medicine in the U.S., believe that regular caffeine use causes physical **dependence**. Heavy caffeine users, Griffiths says, **exhibit** similar behaviors: Their moods **fluctuate** from high to low; they get mild to **severe** headaches; or they feel tired or sad when they can't have a coffee, a soft drink, an energy drink, or a cup of tea. To minimize or stop these feelings, users must consume caffeine—a behavior Griffiths says is characteristic of drug addiction.

Despite these concerns, the general opinion in the scientific community is that caffeine is not dangerous when consumed moderately— for example, having one or two small cups of coffee (about 300 milligrams of caffeine) per day. **Furthermore**, a lot of current research **contradicts** long-held negative beliefs about caffeine, and suggests that it may, in fact, have health benefits. For instance, studies have shown that caffeine can help ease muscle pain. Because it is a stimulant, caffeine can also help improve one's mood. Research has also shown that some caffeinated drinks—specifically certain teas—have disease-fighting chemicals that can help the body fight a number of illnesses, including certain types of cancer.

In addition, as a type of mental stimulant, caffeine increases alertness, memory, and reaction speed. Because it fights fatigue, it **facilitates** performance on tasks like driving, flying, and solving simple math problems. And while it is true that caffeine can increase blood pressure, the effect is usually **temporary** and therefore not likely to cause heart trouble—especially if caffeine is consumed in moderation.[6]

Moreover, despite its nearly universal use, caffeine has rarely been **abused**. "With caffeine, overuse tends to stop itself," says Jack Bergman, a specialist at Harvard Medical School. If you consume too much, "you get . . . uncomfortable, and you don't want to continue."

Caffeine's behavioral effects are real, but most often mild. Getting that burst of energy, of course, is why many of the most popular drinks on Earth contain caffeine. Whether it's a student drinking coffee before class or a businessperson enjoying tea with lunch, humankind's favorite stimulant is at work every day, all over the world.

---

6 If you do something **in moderation** (e.g., smoke or drink), you don't do more than what is reasonable.

A 26-year-old Japanese "cappuccino painter" named Kazuki Yamamoto uses foam to make three-dimensional designs in what coffee fans call "latte art."

Reading Comprehension

Multiple Choice. Choose the best answer for each question.

Gist

1. What is this reading mainly about?
   a. the popularity of coffee
   b. the effects of caffeine on the body
   c. healthy vs. unhealthy caffeine products
   d. the dangers of caffeine intake

Vocabulary

2. In line 5, the word *downing* could be replaced with _____.
   a. holding   b. waking
   c. decreasing   d. drinking

Reference

3. In line 25, *which* refers to _____.
   a. adequate sleep
   b. lack of sleep
   c. food containing caffeine
   d. consuming caffeine

Inference

4. Which statement would sleep expert Charles Czeisler probably agree with?
   a. It's a good idea to consume caffeine if you want to maintain your energy.
   b. Regular consumption of caffeine will make it difficult for you to get enough rest.
   c. How caffeine affects your sleep depends on the type of caffeine you consume.
   d. Caffeine can help you get an adequate amount of sleep if consumed in moderation.

Detail

5. Which of the following is NOT listed as a possible side effect of drinking caffeine?
   a. addiction
   b. mood changes
   c. painful headaches
   d. muscle inflammation

Paraphrase

6. Which of the following is closest in meaning to: *Moreover, despite its nearly universal use, caffeine has rarely been abused.* (lines 77–78)?
   a. Even though caffeine is consumed almost the world over, there aren't many instances of misuse.
   b. Even though caffeine is often misused, it is consumed almost the world over.
   c. Despite caffeine's popularity, addiction isn't a problem.
   d. Caffeine is used all over the world, so it is commonly misused.

Cohesion

7. The following sentence would best be placed at the end of which paragraph? *Many say they couldn't live without it.*
   a. 1 (starting line 1)   b. 4 (starting line 31)
   c. 6 (starting line 50)   d. 8 (starting line 77)

Critical Thinking

Evaluating: Do you think the author is for or against consuming caffeine in day-to-day life? Give reasons to support your ideas.

Discussion: After reading about caffeine, will you change your caffeine consumption in any way? How?

Understanding Pros and Cons

A writer often discusses both sides of an argument or an issue. Understanding the reasons for an issue (the pros) and the reasons against an issue (the cons) helps you evaluate the author's claims and determine your position about the issue. The most effective way to do this is to list the pros and cons in two separate columns. This allows you to determine the strength of each claim.

A. Completion. Look back at the reading on pages 107–108. Complete the chart with the pros and cons of caffeine consumption.

Caffeine consumption	
Pros	**Cons**
• counters _____ fatigue • increases alertness • can help _____ muscle pain • improves mood • can help fight certain illnesses • increases alertness, _____, and reaction speed • improves performance • no serious risk of _____	• causes us to lose _____ • possible risks of cancer and bone disease • can be addictive • causes _____ changes • can cause headaches • going without causes tiredness and _____ • increases _____ temporarily

B. Evaluating. Is eating chocolate good for you? Mark each statement as **P** (a pro) or **C** (a con).

1. _____ It can be expensive if eaten every day.
2. _____ It can cause mood swings.
3. _____ It contains a low level of caffeine, which can help increase alertness.
4. _____ The sugar in chocolate can cause tooth decay.
5. _____ The calcium in chocolate can reduce the harmful effects of tooth decay.
6. _____ It has a lot of calories—just 100 grams contains 520 kcals.

Vocabulary Practice

A. Completion. Complete the information below with the correct form of words from the box. One word is extra.

abuse	**depend**	**exhibit**
facilitate	**furthermore**	**severe**

Did you know that you are **1.** _____ your dog if you feed it chocolate? Too much chocolate can be harmful for dogs and can cause a variety of medical problems. The extent of harm usually **2.** _____ on the type of chocolate. **3.** _____, it is also affected by the amount of chocolate that the dog consumes. Some of the effects are quite **4.** _____, and could possibly lead to death. So if your dog **5.** _____ symptoms such as rapid breathing, or vomiting, it's possible that a chocolate "treat" was the cause.

B. Words in Context. Complete each sentence with the correct answer.

1. If you **facilitate** something, you make it _____.

   a. easier   b. more difficult

2. Something that is **temporary** continues _____.

   a. forever   b. for a limited time

3. A **ritual** is a series of actions or behaviors that is repeated _____.

   a. formally   b. randomly

4. If something is **contradictory**, it _____ another argument.

   a. opposes   b. supports

5. If something **fluctuates**, it _____ a lot in an irregular way.

   a. changes   b. fights

^ A dog begging for chocolate

Thesaurus
furthermore
Also look up:
(*adv.*) *moreover, in addition, as well, on top of that.*

Rows of solar panels collecting sunlight to convert it into energy

Before You Read

A. Discussion. Look at the photo and caption, and answer the questions below.

1. What are some advantages and disadvantages of solar power?

2. Aside from solar power, what are some alternate ways of producing energy?

B. Scan. The passage on pages 113–115 discusses energy sources that are alternatives to fossil fuels. Quickly scan the reading to answer the questions below. Then read to check your ideas.

1. What are the three alternative sources of energy discussed in the passage?

2. Where are these alternative sources of energy commonly used?

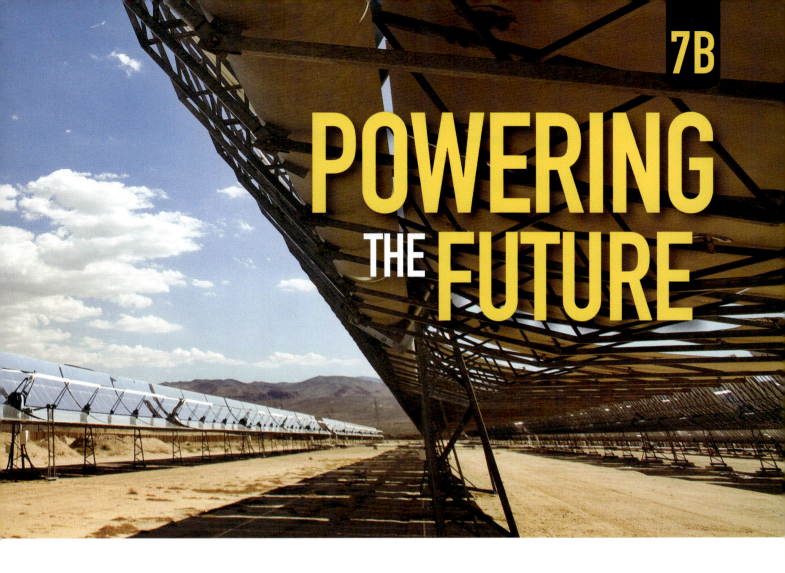

POWERING THE FUTURE

1 Despite modern society's heavy dependence on fossil fuels for energy, most people are aware that the supply of these fuels is finite. As oil, in particular, becomes more costly and difficult to find, researchers are looking at alternative energy sources,

5 including solar, wind, and even nuclear power. But which substitute—if any—is the right one?

Solar

Solar panels catch energy directly from the sun and convert it into electricity. One of the world's largest solar power stations is located near Leipzig, Germany,

10 where more than 33,000 solar panels have the **capacity** to generate enough energy to power about 1,800 homes. But unlike the burning of fossil fuels, the process used to create all that solar energy produces no emissions.

Today, however, solar power provides less than one percent of the world's energy, primarily because the cost of the panels is still very high. And price is only

15 one issue. Clouds and darkness also cause solar panels to produce less energy, which requires one to have additional power sources (such as batteries) available.

^ Windmills on hilltops creating clean green energy, in California, U.S.A.

Some scientists think the solution to this problem can be found in space—which they say is the ideal place to gather energy from the sun.
20 With no clouds and no nighttime, a space-based solar power station could operate constantly. These stations would send the power back to Earth, which could then be turned into electricity for consumption.

25 **Advocates** of solar space stations say this technology would initially require a lot of money, but eventually it could provide continuous, clean energy that would be cheaper than other fuels. Also, unlike other energy
30 sources, solar power from space will last as long as the sun shines, and will be able to **guarantee** everyone on Earth all the energy they need.

Wind

Wind—the fastest-growing alternative energy
35 source—is another way of collecting energy from the sun. Wind is caused by the sun's heat rather than its light, and therefore, unlike solar power, it works well even on cloudy days.

All over Europe, incentives designed to decrease
40 the dependence on oil and coal have led to a **steep** increase in wind-powered energy. Today, Europe leads the world in wind power, producing almost 35,000 megawatts,[1] the **equivalent** of 35 large coal-powered plants.
45 North America remains a distant second, producing just over 7,000 megawatts.

---

1 A **megawatt** is a unit of power.

"This is high-quality landscape . . . They shouldn't be putting those things in here."

Despite its successes, some oppose wind-power development, saying the turbines[2] are both noisy and ugly. Just outside England's Lake District, a protected national park, seven wind towers are planned, each about 40 meters (130 feet) tall. Many locals are protesting. "This is a high-quality landscape," says one local homeowner. "They shouldn't be putting those things in here."

There are other challenges, too. If the wind doesn't blow, the turbines are not able to produce adequate energy. As a result, other power sources are needed. In contrast, a strong wind can create too much power. In cases like this, the energy company must sell the extra power at a much-reduced rate, which is not good for business.

What's needed for both wind and solar is a way to store a large energy surplus.[3] However, most systems are still decades away from making this a reality. On the plus side, both wind and solar enable people to generate their own energy where they live: People can have their own windmills or solar panels, with batteries for calm days.

Nuclear

In the 1970s, nuclear was seen as the main energy alternative. Nuclear power produces vast amounts of electricity more cheaply than gas or coal, with no carbon emissions. For a number of years in the 1980s and '90s, however, use of nuclear power **declined** due to accidents, concerns about nuclear waste storage and **disposal**, and high construction costs.

Today, times are changing. Worldwide, about 432 plants now generate 13 percent of the planet's electric power, and some countries have invested heavily in nuclear energy. France, for instance, gets three quarters of its electricity from nuclear power, the highest of any country. China has started to build one or two new plants a year, and India has also begun to **utilize** nuclear energy on a large scale. However, there are still concerns about the safety of nuclear power, as seen most recently at the Fukushima nuclear power plant in Japan. The country had to close its nuclear reactor when the plant was hit by a tsunami and, as a consequence, began releasing substantial amounts of radioactive materials. Many still believe, however, that nuclear power is one of the future's greenest energy alternatives.

In the end, is any of these sources alone the answer to our current energy problems? The short answer is no, but used in some combination—along with other power sources— we may find ways to reduce and eventually eliminate our dependence on fossil fuels.

---

2 A **turbine** is a machine that uses water, steam, or wind to turn a wheel to produce electricity.

3 If you have a **surplus** of something, you have more of it than you need.

Reading Comprehension

Multiple Choice. Choose the best answer for each question.

Gist

1. What is this reading mainly about?
   a. possible replacements for fossil fuels for energy
   b. the various causes of the energy crisis the world over
   c. the benefits of solar power over other alternate energy sources
   d. problems caused by our overdependence on fossil fuels

Vocabulary

2. In line 12, the word *emissions* is closest in meaning to _____.
   a. panels   b. electricity
   c. pollution   d. accidents

Detail

3. Which of these statements about solar energy is stated in the text?
   a. Solar is currently the biggest contributor to the world's energy.
   b. Solar energy is cheap to produce due to the low price of solar panels.
   c. Solar space stations could be the solution to the energy crisis.
   d. Solar energy can have a harmful effect on the environment.

Detail

4. What is NOT mentioned as a disadvantage of wind power?
   a. Strong winds produce too much power.
   b. Strong winds can damage the turbines.
   c. The turbines create a lot of noise.
   d. The turbines are seen as ugly.

Detail

5. Which of these statements is true about nuclear energy according to the reading?
   a. It is a more expensive form of energy than coal or gas.
   b. It produces a lot of carbon waste.
   c. Safety concerns made nuclear energy unpopular for several decades.
   d. Nuclear energy is becoming less popular than other energy sources.

Detail

6. Which country gets most of its power from nuclear power?
   a. France   b. Germany
   c. India   d. China

Paraphrase

7. Which question is closest in meaning to *In the end, is any of these sources alone the answer to our current energy problems?* (lines 99–100)
   a. Is there an energy source that can solve all of our energy problems on its own?
   b. Can our current energy problems be solved by making sure we stop burning fossil fuel?
   c. Can we solve our energy problems by using all the alternative energy sources together?
   d. Is finding a new alternate to fossil fuels the only way to solve our energy problems?

Critical Thinking

Evaluating: Which of the three energy sources in the article do you think is most likely to replace fossil fuels? Why?

Discussion: Can you think of any other advantages or disadvantages of these energy sources that the writer does not mention?

Using a Venn Diagram to Classify Information

One way to classify information is to organize it in a Venn diagram. These diagrams are used to visually compare and contrast information and to examine relationships. A Venn diagram is made of overlapping circles. Most contain two circles, although some contain three or more.

A. Classification. Work in a group of three. Write your names on the lines in the diagram. Then match each description (**a–g**) with the person(s) it describes. If the information doesn't apply, do not include it.

a. is tall   **e.** is wearing jeans

b. is a student   **f.** likes coffee

c. is male   **g.** can drive

d. has a job

B. Classification. Look back at the reading on pages 113–115. Match each description (**a–g**) with the energy source it describes.

a. fastest-growing energy source today

b. expensive to produce

c. produces no carbon emissions

d. there are safety concerns

e. lack of constant power supply

f. requires a way to store surplus energy to be effective

g. unpopular with nearby residential communities

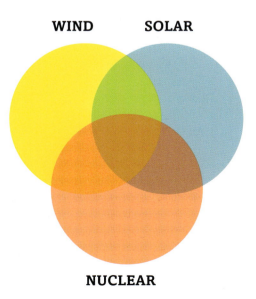

Vocabulary Practice

A. Completion. Complete the information using the words from the box. Three words are extra.

capacity	dispose	equivalent	finite
guarantee	steep	substitute	utilize

The Singapore government, realizing that fossil fuels are a(n) **1.** _____ resource, has decided to **2.** _____ traditional energy production with "renewable energies." As part of this initiative, in 2010, it began to turn Pulau Ubin, a small, undeveloped but inhabited island off the coast of Singapore, into a "green island." The island is now powered entirely by clean and renewable energy, providing the **3.** _____ amount of electricity as it did before, but without using fossil fuels. Residents on the island, who used to **4.** _____ old, inefficient diesel-run generators to supply their power, were pleased to **5.** _____ of them.

Pulau Ubin is part of the Singapore government's plan to move towards renewable energy sources.

B. Words in Context. Complete each sentence with the correct answer.

1. **Advocates** of an idea are _____ it.
   a. for   b. against

2. If a country's energy **capacity** increases, it means _____.
   a. it needs more energy   b. it can produce more energy

3. A country that **utilizes** nuclear power probably _____ nuclear power plants.
   a. has   b. doesn't have any

4. Over the last 100 years, _____ has been **declining**.
   a. environmental quality   b. the world's population

5. A **steep** rise in prices takes place over a _____ period of time.
   a. short   b. long

6. If you **guarantee** that something will happen, you _____ that it will occur.
   a. promise   b. doubt

Word Partnership
Use **steep** with: (n.) steep **hill**, steep **driveway**, steep **increase**, steep **climb**, steep **drop**, steep **fall**.

VIEWING Wave Power

Before You Watch

A. Matching. Scientists and engineers are finding new ways to generate energy from the ocean. Match the captions (1–4) to the correct items in the picture.

1. *Snakes*   Waves move the colorful "snake" up and down, moving the water **pumps** inside.

2. *Kites*   Small underwater **turbines** that are attached, in triangles, to the ocean floor generate power.

3. *Fans*   The changing **tides** move the underwater blades, which act in a similar way to wind turbines.

4. *Paddles*   Floating paddles move up and down, pushing water through high-pressure **pipes** that drive an onshore turbine.

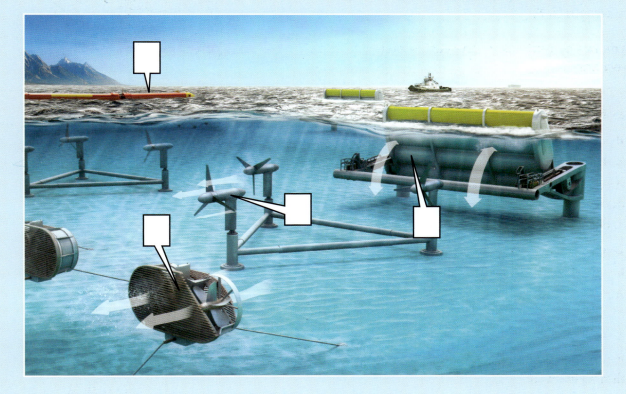

B. Matching. Match the words in **bold** in **A** with their definitions.

_____ long, hollow tubes for carrying water, gas, steam, etc.

_____ devices that force air, water, gas, etc., in or out of something

_____ engines that have parts that turn with the help of water, wind, etc.

_____ the alternating rising and falling of the ocean that occurs each day

While You Watch

A. Main Idea. Check (✓) the main idea of the video.

☐ Power from waves is limitless and holds great promise as an energy source.

☐ Four new machines are changing the way we get our energy from the ocean.

☐ It's easy to generate power from waves, but it's still too expensive.

B. Completion. Complete each sentence with the correct answer.

1. Richard Yemm describes the wave power opportunities as (**unlimited / effective**).
2. Pelamis moves (**back and forth / up and down**) in the water.
3. (**Tides / Waves**) cause Pelamis to move, which generates energy.
4. The first commercial customer for Pelamis was in (**Scotland / Portugal**).
5. Yemm describes Pelamis's features as (**adaptable / survivable**).
6. When Pelamis was being tested, a (**turbine / pump**) stopped working.

After You Watch

A. Discussion. Discuss these questions with a partner.

1. What are some possible disadvantages of generating power from ocean waves and tides?
2. From what you have learned in this unit, which do you think has the most potential—solar, wind, nuclear, or wave power?

Answers to Before You Read, page 106:
1. b; **2.** a; **3.** c; **4.** e; **5.** g; **6.** d; **7.** h; **8.** f

8

EPIC
ENGINEERING

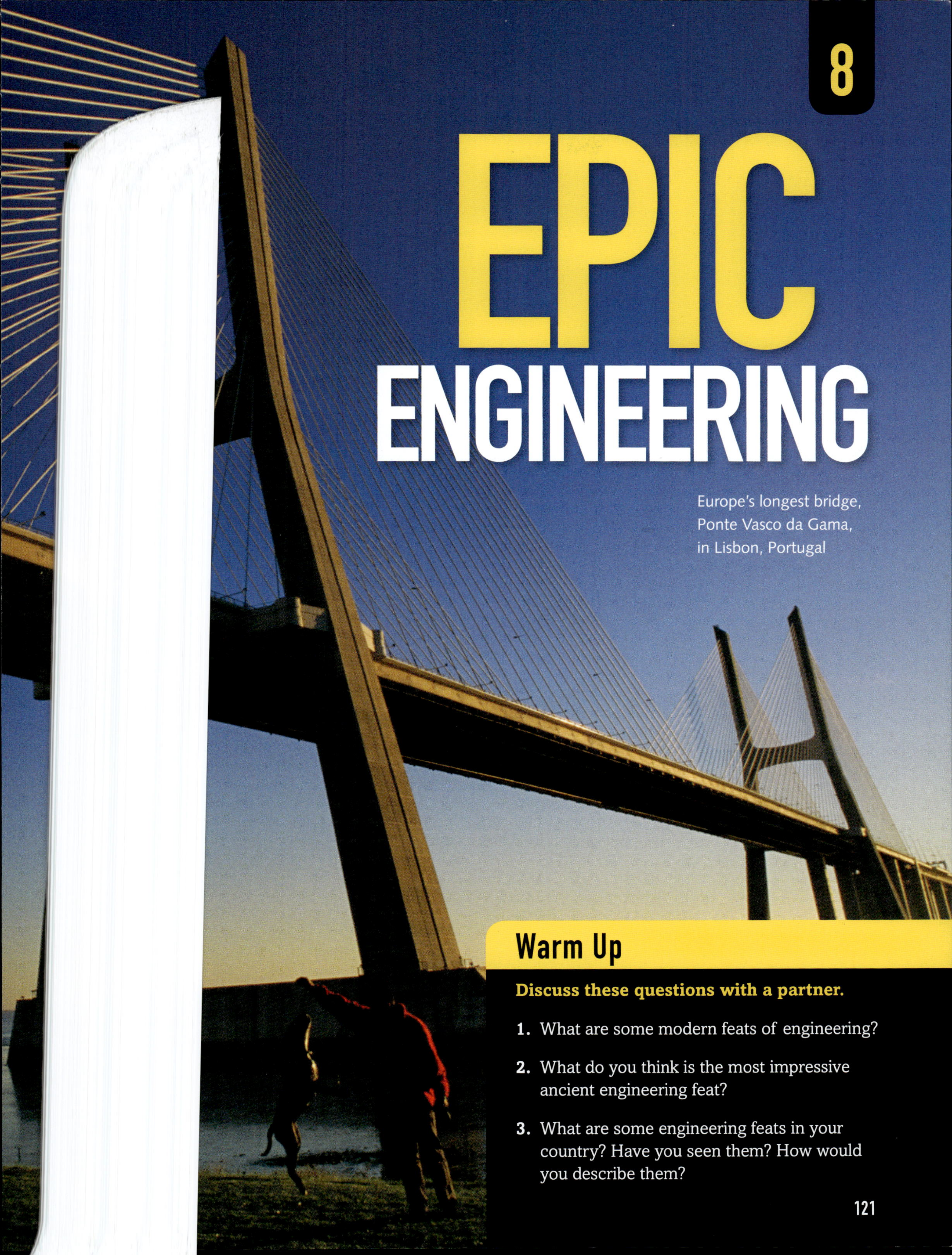

Europe's longest bridge,
Ponte Vasco da Gama,
in Lisbon, Portugal

Warm Up

Discuss these questions with a partner.

1. What are some modern feats of engineering?

2. What do you think is the most impressive ancient engineering feat?

3. What are some engineering feats in your country? Have you seen them? How would you describe them?

121

The Grand Canal, shown here passing through the city of Jining, is a large waterway that first connected north and south China over 1,400 years ago. It is still in use today.

Before You Read

A. **Scanning.** Look at the pictures and maps, and read the captions on pages 123–126. Discuss the questions with a partner.

1. Where is the Grand Canal, and when was it built?

2. What are some of the ways a canal like this might be used?

3. What were its northernmost and southernmost cities?

4. How long is the Grand Canal today? What is its northernmost city now?

B. **Predict.** For what reasons do you think the Grand Canal has been important for China? Share your ideas with a partner. Then read the passage to check your ideas.

CHINA'S
GRAND CANAL

the power of Chinese emperors rose and fell with their control of
nal. Today, this important waterway is shorter than it once was,
he longest man-made river in the world, and continues to play an
tural and economic role in modern China.

on Begins

al system began around the
mperor Yang realized that—
is army—he needed a way
ckly from China's southern

10   rice-growing region to the country's north. An
estimated one million people, mostly farmers,
worked to build the first section of the Grand
Canal, which connected existing canals, lakes,
and rivers. Construction took six years and was
15   completed in 611.

Over the next 500 years, the canal's importance grew throughout China, but by 1127, parts were deteriorating.[1] In 1279, Kublai Khan began to **repair** and build new parts of the canal. This **renovation** created a more direct north–south route to and from Beijing. Future rulers then continued to expand and improve the canal.

A Nation's Lifeline

In addition to moving rice around China, the Grand Canal was also an important cultural conduit.[2] Soldiers, merchants, and artists **transported** ideas, **regional** foods, and cultural practices from one part of China to another along the country's watery highway. According to legend, this is how Beijing **acquired** two of its best-known trademarks: Peking[3] duck, a dish from Shandong Province in the south, and Peking opera, from Anhui and Hubei, also in the south.

---

1 If something **deteriorates**, it gets worse in some way.

2 A **conduit** is something that connects two or more people, places, or things.

3 **Peking** is the former name for Beijing.

⌄ Chinese opera performers prepare for a festival in Macao, China

Beijing

Grand Canal

...al was ...ars ago ...cultural ...with the political ... is in the north. For centuries, the canal ran 1,770 kilometers (1,100 miles) between Beijing and the southern city of Hangzhou, transporting everything from food to wood and textiles.

Tianjin

Cangzhou

Bo Hai

Dezhou

Linqing

Mt. Tai
5,000 ft
1,524 m

Jining

Yellow

Yellow
Sea

Yellow

Huaiyin

Huai

Yangzhou

Yangtze

China's last dynasty, the Qing, took control in 1644. Emperor Qinglong (above) made six inspection tours of the Grand Canal, visiting different ports and cultural sites, like the Buddhist temple on Tiger Hill in Suzhou.

Changzhou

Suzhou

▲ Tiger Hill

Hangzhou

For almost four decades, the path from Beijing to Jining has been too dry for shipping. Today, the Grand Canal's main route runs 523 kilometers (325 miles) from Jining to Hangzhou.

The Modern Canal

For more than a thousand years, goods have been transported along the Grand Canal. Even today, the country's watery highway plays an
40   important economic role in China. Boats continue to carry tons of coal, food, and other goods to points between Hangzhou and Jining. In addition, local governments—eager to increase tourism and real estate[4] development—are working to
45   beautify areas along the canal.

This development comes at a price, though. In Yangzhou, the city has torn down almost all of the older canal-side buildings. Farther south in the cities of Zhenjiang, Wuxi, and Hangzhou, the
50   situation is similar. In Hangzhou, for example, almost all of the ancient buildings have been **demolished**. "Traditionally we talk about 18 main cities on the Grand Canal, and each had something unique and special about it," explains

55   Zhou Xinhua, the **former** vice director of the Grand Canal museum in Hangzhou. "But now many of these cities are all the same: a thousand people with one face."

In 2005, a group of **citizens** proposed that the
60   historic Grand Canal be made a UNESCO World Heritage site,[5] to protect both the waterway and the architecture around it. "Every generation wants the next generation to understand it, to look at its monuments," said Zhu Bingren, an
65   artist who cowrote this proposal. The hope is that the Grand Canal, a site of cultural and economic importance—and one of the world's great engineering accomplishments—will continue to link north and south China for centuries to come.

---

4 **Real estate** is property in the form of land and buildings.
5 A **UNESCO World Heritage site** is a place that's listed by UNESCO (United Nations Educational, Scientific and Cultural Organization) as having special cultural or physical significance.

Multiple Choice. Choose the best answer for each question.

Detail

1. Why was the Grand Canal originally built?
   a. to allow the army to move quickly from the north to the south
   b. to transport food from the southern regions of China to the northern regions
   c. to enable more people to visit remote parts of China
   d. to promote the cultural and traditional diversity of the south of China

Detail

2. What is NOT true about the Grand Canal?
   a. It originally took six years to complete its construction.
   b. Even today, it is the largest man-made river in the world.
   c. Around a million people worked on the first section of the canal.
   d. It allowed Peking duck and Peking opera to spread to southern China.

Main Idea

3. What would be the best alternative heading for the fourth paragraph (starting line 24)?
   a. Renewed Importance
   b. Cultural Connections
   c. The Army's Highway
   d. The Origins of Peking Opera

Vocabulary

4. In line 29, the word *practices* could be replaced with _____.
   a. traditions
   b. repetitions
   c. instructions
   d. improvements

Paraphrase

5. Which of the following is closest in meaning to *This development comes at a price, though.* (line 46)?
   a. But developing the canal involves spending a lot of money.
   b. But even after spending money, people might not like the development.
   c. But developing it is a lot more expensive than one can imagine.
   d. But there are some negative consequences to having this development.

Inference

6. The artist Zhu Bingren would probably most like to see that _____.
   a. the canal and the area around it are declared a heritage site
   b. the canal is further expanded in an east–west direction
   c. more changes are made to modernize the canal
   d. a monument is created to honor China's economic and cultural importance

Cohesion

7. The following sentence would best be placed at the end of which paragraph? *The city of Yangzhou, for example, has created a beautiful park near its waterfront.*
   a. 1 (starting line 1)
   b. 4 (starting line 25)
   c. 5 (starting line 37)
   d. 7 (starting line 59)

Critical Thinking

Interpreting: What does Zhou Xinhua mean when he says, "... now many of these cities are all the same: a thousand people with one face."

_____

Discussion: What do you think the Grand Canal will be like in the future? Why?

Understanding Compound Words

Compound words are made when two (or more) words are put together to create a new word. To understand the meaning of a compound word, break it into its parts and look at the meaning of the individual words. Compound words can be a single word (e.g., *waterway*), two words (e.g., *real estate*), or two words linked by a hyphen (e.g., *man-made*).

A. Definitions. Scan the heading and paragraph (starting line 25) on page 124. Find and underline the compound words. Then write them next to their definitions.

1. _____ : most widely recognized

2. _____ : a road that connects two towns or cities

3. _____ : something a person or place is known for

4. _____ : something that provides help or support needed for survival

B. Completion. Join words from the two boxes, and write the compound words in the correct sentences. Use a dictionary to help you.

A section of the Great Wall at the Hebei-Beijing border, China

day	man
high	well
life	with

known	out
light	time
made	trip

In addition to the Grand Canal, China is **1.** _____ for another **2.** _____ wonder—the Great Wall. China's first emperor wanted a wall for protection. **3.** _____ a wall, his country was vulnerable to attack from the north. Construction began during the first emperor's **4.** _____, but work continued for many hundreds of years after his death. Each emperor added to the wall to protect his power. Construction continued until the wall was thousands of kilometers long. Today, the Great Wall still stands. It can be easily visited on a **5.** _____ from Beijing and is a **6.** _____ for many locals and international visitors.

Vocabulary Practice

A. Completion. Complete the information by circling the correct word in each pair.

One of the world's greatest engineering achievements, the 77-kilometer (48-mile) Panama Canal links the Atlantic and Pacific Oceans. The United States **1. (repaired / acquired)** the canal project from the French in the early 19th century. Its completion in 1914 shortened a ship's voyage between New York City and San Francisco by 8,370 kilometers (5,200 miles). The canal helped fuel trade and **2. (former / economic)** growth in countries dependent on shipping.

Although traffic has continued to increase over the years, many of today's ships could not fit through the **3. (original / regional)** canal. A $5.2 billion **4. (renovation / citizen)** and expansion project now allows much larger ships to pass through the canal. This has led to a sharp increase in the amount of goods that can be **5. (demolished / transported)** through the canal. Today, more than 14,000 ships pass through the Panama Canal every year.

∧ Miraflores Locks, on the Panama Canal

B. Words in Context. Complete each sentence with the correct answer.

1. If you **repair** a computer, you _____ it.
   a. clean   b. fix
2. A **former** president is a _____ president.
   a. past   b. future
3. A **citizen** of a country _____ the legal rights of that country.
   a. has   b. does not have
4. If you **demolish** a bridge, you _____ it.
   a. build   b. destroy
5. A **regional** language is spoken in _____ a country.
   a. a particular area of   b. all parts of

Word Link The word root **nov** means *new*, e.g., *renovate, innovate, novel, novice, nova.*

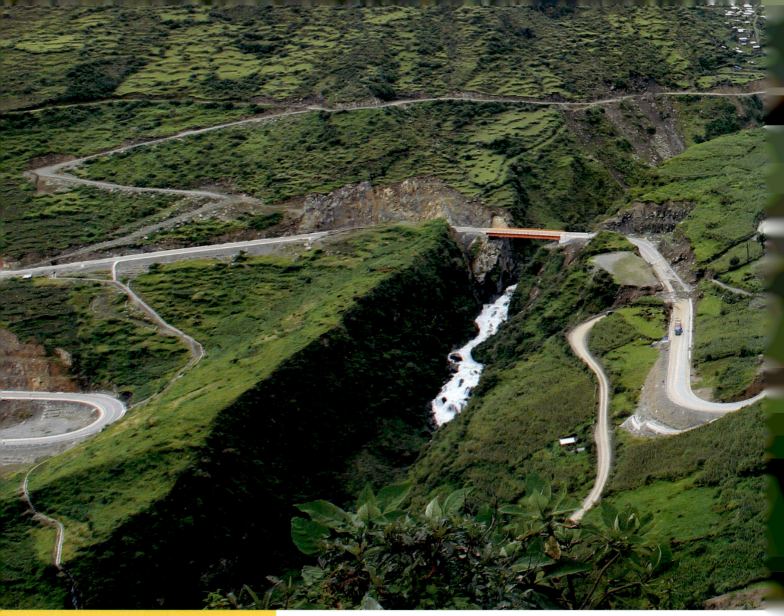

▲ This road is part of a new 2,600-kilometer (1,600-mile) Transoceanic Highway. The highway stretches from the Pacific Ocean in Peru and connects with Brazil's already existing highways, which travel to the Atlantic.

Before You Read

A. Discussion. Read the caption and answer the questions with a partner.

1. Many Peruvians are happy about the construction of the Transoceanic Highway. Why do you think this is?

   _____

   _____

2. What concerns might environmentalists have about the highway?

   _____

   _____

B. Scan. Scan the reading on pages 131–133, and underline any answers to the two questions above. Then read the passage closely to check your ideas.

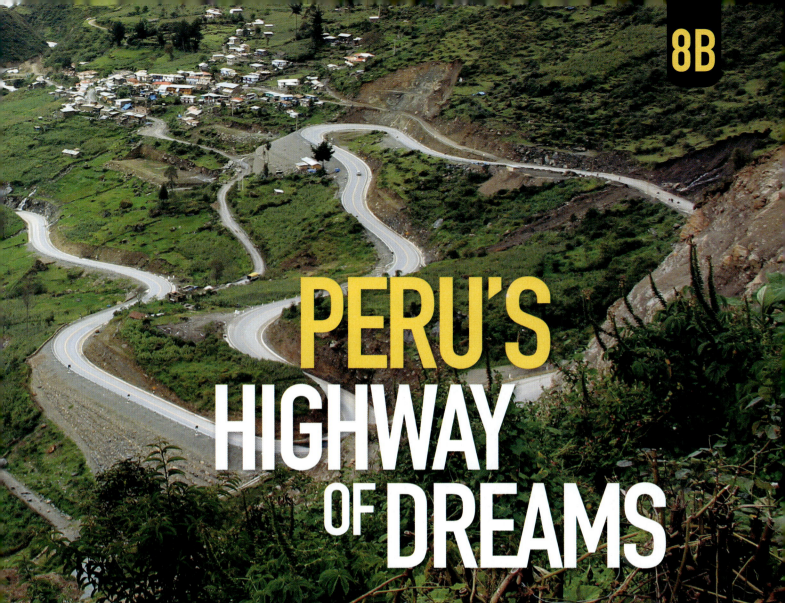

PERU'S HIGHWAY OF DREAMS

1   A new road that connects the Pacific with the Atlantic could bring riches—and environmental **ruin**.

   Mary Luz Guerra remembers a trip she took in 2003 from
5   the city of Cusco, high in the Peruvian Andes, to her home in Puerto Maldonado, a city in the Amazon rain forest. By plane, this 320-kilometer (200-mile) journey would have taken only 37 minutes, but Mary Luz had traveled by truck: along narrow mountain roads, across rushing
10 rivers, and through **dense** Amazon jungle. It took her three days to reach home. During the long and exhausting trip, she remembers thinking, "I can't wait till they build that highway!" Almost ten years after that impossibly long journey, Mary Luz's wish came true.

Bridging a Continent

In early 2012, the Transoceanic Highway opened to public vehicles for the first time. A dream of Peru's leaders since the 1950s, work on the vast network of roads and bridges began in 2006 and was completed in late 2011. Today, the east–west passageway spans 2,600 kilometers (1,600 miles). From Peru's Pacific Ocean coastline, it continues across the Andes Mountains and through a large part of the Amazon rain forest in the Peruvian state of Madre de Dios. It then travels into Brazil, where it connects with a network of existing highways to the Atlantic.

The Transoceanic Highway has been celebrated as one of South America's greatest engineering feats, and supporters say it will greatly improve people's lives. Until recently, travel between the cities of Cusco and Puerto Maldonado in Peru took days by bus or truck—as Mary Luz's story **illustrates**—and drivers had to use narrow, **partially** unpaved[1] mountain roads. Now, thanks to the new highway, the trip only takes a few hours, and is much safer.

Improving People's Lives

In addition to making travel faster and easier, supporters say the highway will also be good for business. There is **enormous** demand in North America and Asia for Brazilian and Peruvian products, including soybeans, beef, and gold. A number of companies in Cusco and Puerto Maldonado also sell wood to different corners of the world. Many of these companies transport their lumber[2] to the Pacific, where it travels by ship to other countries. Thanks to the highway, wood can now reach the Pacific in days; in the

---

1 If a road is **unpaved**, it is mostly dirt.
2 **Lumber** is wood that has been cut into boards.

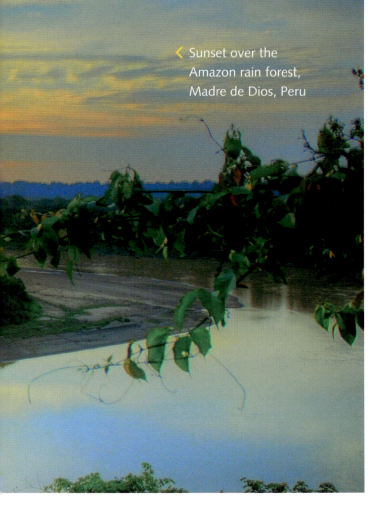

< Sunset over the Amazon rain forest, Madre de Dios, Peru

past, it could take a week or more. This lowers costs and allows the wood to reach a company's **customers** sooner, and also in better condition. In the long run, say many business owners, this will mean more profit.

The highway will also open up areas of the Peruvian Amazon that were **inaccessible** just a few years ago. The highway may increase activity in these areas and give people new places to live and travel to. This, in turn, could mean more jobs and money for Peruvians.

Environmental Challenges

Despite the highway's many potential benefits, environmentalists are concerned. The Transoceanic passes directly through a large part of the Amazon rain forest, in the state of Madre de Dios in Peru. According to a Peruvian government study, the forested area in the western mountains of this state has the greatest biodiversity[3] of any place on Earth, and until recently, large parts of the forest were in pristine[4] condition. As more people are moving into the region, environmentalists are worrying about the **impact** this will have on the Amazon's plants and animals, many of which are found nowhere else.

Shortly after the highway opened, large numbers of people began coming into Puerto Maldonado from all over Peru—and the world—to mine gold. There's a lot of money to be made in mining, as well as in farming, says environmental photographer Gabby Salazar. "I think we're going to see a big increase in farming," she says. "Right across the border in Brazil, you see soybean farms all over the place." Studies show three-quarters of the deforestation[5] of the Brazilian Amazon **occurs** within 50 kilometers (30 miles) of a highway, and environmentalists like Salazar are concerned that the same thing will happen in Peru. "It's having an impact on the environment," she explains. "It's having an impact on the people as well."

Faced with these risks, many Peruvians talk about the importance of being **practical**. "In rural[6] Peru, a lot of people are living in poverty, so it's very difficult to say don't build the highway," explains Roger Mustalish, president of the Amazon Center for Environmental Education and Research. "But every time you see a road like this going through, you soon see major changes." Will these changes be mostly positive or negative? Many Peruvians are hopeful, but only time will tell.

---

3 **Biodiversity** is the existence of a wide variety of living things (plants, animals, insects, etc.) in a certain place.

4 If something is **pristine**, it is in its original condition or is unspoiled.

5 **Deforestation** is the destruction or cutting down of all the trees in an area.

6 **Rural** places are in the country, far away from cities.

Reading Comprehension

Multiple Choice. Choose the best answer for each question.

Gist **1.** What is the reading mainly about?
  a. the impact a highway will have on the environment and people of Peru
  b. how the Brazilian government helped the people of Peru build a new highway
  c. a new development that is resulting in mining and farming jobs
  d. how environmentalists are protecting the Amazon's diverse wildlife

Detail **2.** What is true about the Transoceanic Highway?
  a. Its construction began in the 1950s.
  b. It helps connect the Pacific Ocean with Brazil.
  c. It was opened to the public in 2006.
  d. It begins at the Atlantic Ocean.

Vocabulary **3.** The phrase *In the long run* (line 53) could be replaced by _____.
  a. on the other hand
  b. as expected
  c. eventually
  d. optimistically

Detail **4.** What is NOT given as a reason the highway will be good for Peru?
  a. The cost of transporting goods will be lower.
  b. Goods will reach customers in better condition.
  c. It will increase the number of tourists in Peru.
  d. Goods will reach customers faster.

Detail **5.** Which of the following concerns does the reading specifically mention?
  a. Increased mining will lead to soil erosion.
  b. Farming will lead to an increase in water pollution.
  c. The highway will have an impact on plants and animals.
  d. The cities along the highway will become overpopulated.

Reference **6.** In line 92 , what does *these risks* refer to?
  a. environmental risks
  b. financial risks
  c. transportation risks
  d. depopulation risks

Main Idea **7.** What would be the best heading for the final paragraph?
  a. A Positive Future
  b. Finding the Right Balance
  c. An End to Poverty
  d. Say No to Highways

Critical Thinking

Evaluating: Who do you think the Transoceanic Highway will benefit the most? In what way?

_____

Discussion: Think of a large construction project in your country. Do you think the advantages outweighed the disadvantages?

Organizing Notes in a T-chart

One way to organize your notes about a reading is to use a T-chart.
A T-chart is particularly useful when you need to examine two aspects
of a topic. For example, a T-chart can be used to note similarities and
differences, compare advantages and disadvantages, show problems
and solutions, evaluate pros and cons, or separate facts from opinions.

A. **Analyzing.** Look at the following types of texts. Check (✓) the three
   in which you would probably use a T-chart to organize your notes.

   1. ☐ a list of tips for getting into the top college in the country

   2. ☐ a comparison of pursuing a science degree vs. pursuing an
        arts degree

   3. ☐ an article about how a neighborhood fought back against an
        increase in crime

   4. ☐ a blog post about a guided food tour of a Paris market

   5. ☐ an article about problems caused by crime in a neighborhood
        and some possible solutions

   6. ☐ a summary of why a community is divided over the
        construction of a new shopping mall

B. **Completion.** Look back at the reading on pages 131–133.
   Complete the T-chart with words from the text.

How the highway may help	How the highway may harm
• _f_____, safer, and easier travel	• crosses an area high in _b_____
• _b_____ for business	• crosses an area in pristine _c_____
• gives people new areas to _l_____ in and travel to	• has _i_____ on plants, animals, and people
• more _j_____ and more money for locals	• leads to deforestation from mining and _f_____

Vocabulary Practice

A. Completion. Complete the information by circling the correct word in each pair.

For the past decade, engineers have been at work deep under the Swiss Alps, building a(n) **1. (enormous / practical)** tunnel. Although only **2. (partially / densely)** completed, the Gotthard Base Tunnel will be the world's longest and deepest railway tunnel when it opens in 2017. Once that **3. (illustrates / occurs)**, high-speed trains will travel through the Alps at 250 kilometers (155 miles) per hour.

In the last few decades, a huge number of trucks crossing the Alps have had an enormous **4. (customer / impact)** on the environment. The new tunnel provides a(n) **5. (practical / inaccessible)** solution to this problem. Goods will be transported by train between northern and southern Europe, without **6. (illustrating / ruining)** the beautiful mountain landscape.

B. Definitions. Use the correct form of words in **A** to complete the definitions.

1. A(n) _____ jungle has many plants in it.

2. If something has been _____, it has been broken and destroyed.

3. People who buy goods and services from a business are its _____.

4. If something is _____, it is difficult or impossible to reach.

5. If something _____ another thing, it serves as an example of that thing.

A village in the
Swiss Alps

> At 57 kilometers (35 miles) long, the Gotthard Base Tunnel will be the world's longest railway tunnel.

Word Partnership
Use *dense* with:
dense **jungle**, dense **forest**, dense **fog**, dense **vegetation**.

VIEWING Birth of a Rain Forest

Before You Watch

A. Labeling. Look at the picture and read a description of a "Green Museum." Use the words in **bold** to label the parts of the picture (1–5).

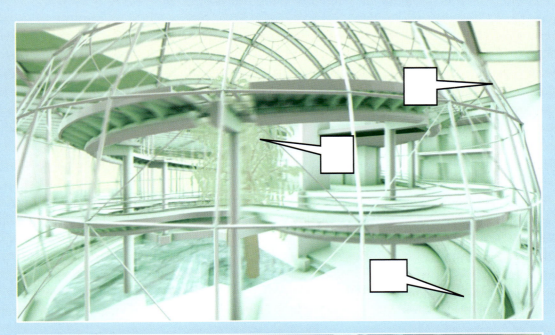

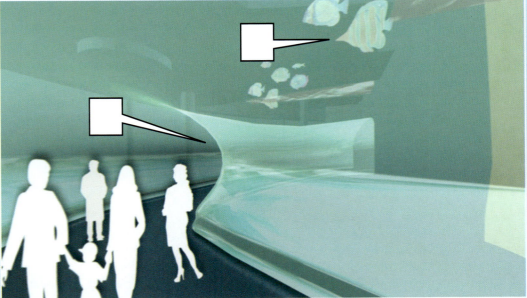

Guests will walk up a spiral **1. ramp**, inside the glass **2. dome**, all the way up through the trees to the **3. canopy**, to parts of the tree that would normally be inaccessible. Then they ride a glass elevator all the way down to a **4. tunnel** under the rain forest. Here, they can see the marine animals in the **5. aquarium**.

While You Watch

A. Noticing. The rain forest exhibit and aquarium will contain many different types of animals. Circle all the animals that are mentioned.

birds   monkeys   stingrays   insects   fish

sharks   butterflies   turtle   whales   snakes

B. Multiple Choice. Choose the best answer for each question.

1. What is true about the California Academy of Sciences?

    a. It's in Los Angeles.

    b. It gets 20 million visitors a year.

    c. It's the largest green museum in the world.

2. What does Chris Andrews say about the rain forest exhibit?

    a. There will be two of every animal.

    b. It will feel and smell like a real rain forest.

    c. It will be as good as replacing nature.

3. Who is Diego?

    a. a turtle

    b. the first visitor

    c. Chris Andrews' assistant

After You Watch

A. Discussion. Work in a group. Imagine you want to create a green museum. Discuss the following questions.

1. What would the place look like?

2. What plants and animals would you include?

3. Where and how would you display them?

Now, in your groups, draw a plan of your museum and label all the important features. How is the architecture of your museum similar to or different from the one you just saw?

⌄ Innovative indoor forest exhibits can now be found in other cities, such as Singapore's Gardens by the Bay.

9

FAR OUT

A view of Earth from the International Space Station (ISS)

Warm Up

Discuss these questions with a partner.

1. What are some reasons humans explore space?

2. What has been humankind's greatest achievement in space exploration?

3. What are some of the dangers involved with space travel? How can we avoid them?

DEFYING GRAVITY

A. Scan and Discuss. Look at the photo, study the caption on page 141, and answer the questions.

1. What are the astronauts doing in the photo? Where are they?

2. What do you think this station is used for?

3. What do you think is the best part of working at the ISS? What do you think are the biggest challenges?

B. Skim and Predict. Look quickly at pages 141–143. What do you expect to learn about in this reading? Check (✓) your answers. Then read the passage to check your ideas.

- ☐ the history of walking in space
- ☐ how a person becomes an astronaut
- ☐ some common problems at the ISS
- ☐ how astronauts prepare for a spacewalk
- ☐ possible dangers of spacewalking
- ☐ one astronaut's experience in space

Astronauts working outside the International Space Station (ISS). The ISS is a permanent space laboratory about 380 kilometers (235 miles) above Earth.

1　Italian astronaut Luca Parmitano had a terrifying experience during a spacewalk. While working on the International Space Station (ISS), his helmet[1] began filling with water.

5　At first, Parmitano wasn't sure what it was. "My head is really wet," he told NASA flight controllers back on Earth. As the water began to **accumulate**, Parmitano realized there was a problem. "It's too much . . . Now it's in my eyes," he recalls saying. **Concerned** that he might choke[2] on the water, ground control stopped the spacewalk. Back inside the ISS,
10　Parmitano took off his helmet and discovered that it contained almost half a liter (two cups) of water. Where had this water come from?

---

1 A **helmet** is a hat made of strong material that often covers the face as well; it protects your head.
2 If you **choke** on something, you cannot breathe because something is stuck in your throat.

NASA found out that a malfunction[3] in the suit's liquid cooling system had caused water to leak. Some of the water got into Parmitano's helmet. Though NASA has taken steps to correct the problem, the experience **underscores** the dangers that astronauts face each time they **venture** outside a spacecraft.

Training for a Spacewalk

Spacewalks are safer now than they were fifty years ago, when—in 1965—Russian Alexei Leonov carried out the first one. However, as Parmitano's experience illustrates, there are still risks involved. To ensure that missions are successful, astronauts train for hundreds of hours on Earth. They learn to deal with the lack of gravity in space, for example, by **floating** in a large tank[4] of water, where they experience a feeling very close to the weightlessness of space. For every hour they will walk in space, astronauts practice for ten hours in the water. They also **familiarize** themselves with the exact route they will take once they leave a spacecraft. They repeatedly go over this path so they know exactly what to do on a spacewalk.

Astronauts also train for emergencies that may come about during a walk. One of the most common is losing **consciousness**. Although spacesuits have an internal heating and cooling system, they can still get very hot, especially when astronauts are doing physically **demanding** work outside the spacecraft for hours. Astronauts are trained to monitor their breathing and to make sure their bodies aren't getting overheated, which could cause them to pass out. Another potential challenge that astronauts are trained to deal with is being separated from a spacecraft. During a walk, astronauts work in pairs and are attached to the ISS for safety reasons. Every NASA spacesuit has a mini jet pack, and astronauts are trained to use it to float back to the station if they somehow become detached from the craft.

---

3 A **malfunction** is a failure to work normally.
4 A **tank** is a large container that holds liquid (like water) or gas.

SPACEWALKER:

SUNITA WILLIAMS

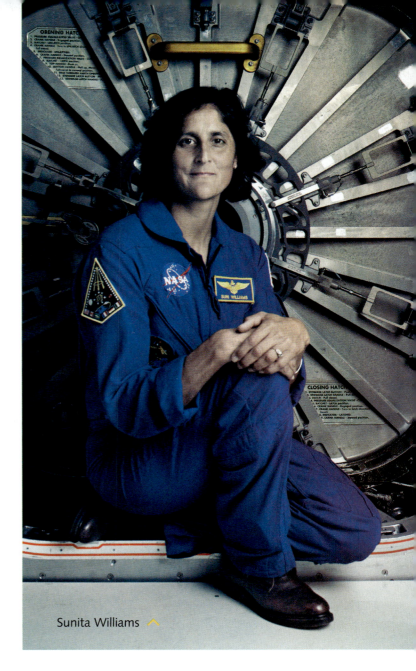

Sunita Williams

As a child, Sunita Williams believed that space travel would be routine when she grew up—something everyone did. She never thought she'd be one of the **pioneers**. The former pilot has visited the International Space Station four times and has spent 50 hours walking in space—the most spacewalking of any female astronaut.

National Geographic: What's the most **impressive** thing about a spacewalk?

Sunita Williams: The view—being up very high looking down and seeing the northern lights below.

NG: Is it scary?

Sunita Williams: On my first walk in 2006, there was a problem with a solar array (a solar panel) on the station, and we needed to fix it. A long arm connects the space station to the array. As I started going up this arm to the array, I felt like I was climbing a skyscraper. I had to tell myself, "It's OK. You're not going to fall." In space, you can get really confused sometimes. You don't know if you are going up or down, left or right. During that first walk outside the ISS, I had to remind myself how we trained in the water tank. That helped me stay calm.

NG: Are there things you do to keep yourself grounded[5] while living in space?

Sunita Williams: On my first flight, I would go down to the Russian end of the space station because there was only one bathroom at the time. Astronaut Misha Tyurin would always say, "Would you like some tea?" We would sit or float in the air for five or ten minutes drinking tea and just talk about life.

---

[5] If you are **grounded**, you behave in a calm, sensible way, like a normal person.

Reading Comprehension

Multiple Choice. Choose the best answer for each question.

Cause and Effect
1. What caused Luca Parmitano's helmet to fill with water?
   a. There was a crack in his helmet, which caused a leak.
   b. A bag with drinking water inside his suit began to leak.
   c. No one knows why it filled with water.
   d. There was a problem with his suit's liquid cooling system.

Detail
2. Who was the first person to go on a spacewalk?
   a. Luca Parmitano
   b. Alexei Leonov
   c. Sunita Williams
   d. Misha Tyurin

Detail
3. How long does an astronaut need to practice in the water to prepare for a two-hour spacewalk?
   a. ten hours
   b. twenty hours
   c. thirty hours
   d. hundreds of hours

Detail
4. What is NOT mentioned as part of spacewalk training?
   a. dealing with weightlessness
   b. communicating with the ship
   c. becoming familiar with the route
   d. what to do in an emergency

Reference
5. What does *it* refer to in line 52?
   a. the walk
   b. the spacecraft
   c. the jet pack
   d. the spacesuit

Detail
6. What is NOT true about Sunita Williams?
   a. She has visited the ISS four times.
   b. She has spacewalked for more than 40 hours.
   c. She once thought traveling into space would be a common thing.
   d. She always believed she would be a space pioneer.

Detail
7. What experience does Sunita Williams describe as being scary?
   a. returning to Earth
   b. training in a water tank
   c. falling off a solar panel
   d. climbing up to a solar array

Critical Thinking

Evaluating: Which of the challenges mentioned in the reading do you think would be the most difficult to deal with? Give reasons for your answers.

Discussion: In what ways are spacewalkers similar to, and different from, other kinds of risk-takers mentioned in Unit 6?

Recognizing Phrasal Verbs

Phrasal verbs are usually two-word (but sometimes three-word) phrases that consist of a verb + preposition or adverb. Adding a preposition or an adverb creates a different meaning from the original verb. Phrasal verbs are very common in spoken English, but examples can also be found in written English. Their meaning is usually not obvious and so may need to be memorized.

A. Definitions. Look back at the reading on pages 141–143. Find and write the phrasal verbs that match these definitions.

1. remove (page 141) _____

2. discovered (page 142) _____

3. performed (page 142) _____

4. handle; manage (page 142) _____

5. occur (page 142) _____

6. faint (page 142) _____

7. became an adult (page 143) _____

B. Completion. Circle the correct word to complete each phrasal verb. Check the words in a dictionary.

Sunita Williams may be a spacewalker, but she is also a space runner. While on the ISS in 2007, Williams **1.** took part **at / in / with** the Boston Marathon, **2.** finishing **off / down / through** the 42-kilometer (26.2-mile) race in 4 hours, 23 minutes, and 10 seconds.

Unlike runners on Earth, who had to **3.** deal **of / with / forward** strong winds and rain, Williams stayed dry. She started running on a treadmill as the race **4.** kicked **off / to / on** in Boston and the ISS circled Earth at about 28,000 kilometers (17,400 miles) an hour. Her fellow astronauts **5.** cheered her **with / on / over**.

"I think the idea **6.** came **out / up / away** because I'm a big proponent[1] of physical fitness," Williams told reporters during a video interview.

---

1 If you are a **proponent** of something, you argue in favor of that thing.

Vocabulary Practice

A. Completion. Complete the information below with words from the box. One word is extra.

accumulated	**demanding**	**familiarize**
floating	**impressive**	**venture**

Before they can **1.** _____ into space, astronauts on the ISS have to undergo a very

2. _____ training. First, they have to pass a one-year course of basic training in which they learn about space technology, medical skills, and how the ISS works. They also **3.** _____ themselves with scuba diving so they can get used to the feeling of

4. _____ in space. After they have

5. _____ the required number of training hours, they can then be assigned to a mission.

B. Definitions. Use the correct form of words in the box to complete the definitions.

consciousness	**concerned**	**impressive**
pioneer	**underscore**	**venture**

1. You admire or respect something that is
   _____.

2. A _____ is somebody who is the first to do something.

3. If something _____ something else, it emphasizes or stresses it.

4. If something _____ you, it makes you feel uneasy or anxious about it.

5. You _____ into a place when you go somewhere dangerous or exciting.

6. _____ is the normal state of being awake and aware of your surroundings.

∧ Astronauts in training get used to the feeling of weightlessness by repeatedly climbing and diving in a jet.

Word Link The suffix **-ize**, meaning "cause" or "become," can be added to some words to make verbs, e.g., *familiarize, popularize, standardize, modernize, socialize.*

THE ULTIMATE TRIP

Before You Read

The spacecraft Curiosity heads toward the planet Mars in this illustration from NASA.

A. Quiz. Below are some key events in the history of space exploration. Match each event with a year. Then check your answers on pages 150–151.

1. _____ The U.S.A. lands the first spacecraft on the moon.   **a.** 1961
2. _____ The privately funded manned ship SpaceShipOne goes into space.   **b.** 1969
3. _____ The first space shuttle, Columbia, is launched.   **c.** 1981
4. _____ The International Space Station is established.   **d.** 1998
5. _____ The first space tourist visits the ISS.   **e.** 2001
6. _____ Soviet astronaut Yuri Gagarin is the first human in space.   **f.** 2004

B. Predict. What will be some important events in space travel and exploration in the future? Check your ideas as you read the passage.

In this artist's impression, an unmanned probe explores a new solar system.

THOUGH WE HAVE sent unmanned[1] spacecraft to Mars and other parts of our solar system for **decades**, humans haven't ventured more than 650 kilometers (400 miles) from Earth since 1973. However, there is increasing interest in sending new missions—both robotic and manned— into space. But unlike in the past, this renewed interest is not primarily being driven by government agencies. Instead, private companies are leading today's new age of space exploration.

Take, for example, SpaceX, a private company based near Los Angeles. In early 2012, it sent an unmanned rocket to the International Space Station (ISS). Until now, astronauts and supplies from the U.S. have been transported by space shuttle to the ISS. SpaceX and other companies are competing to **replace** the U.S. government shuttle and become the ISS's supply ship.

Another company called Planetary Resources— which is **backed** by billionaires from Google— plans to use robotic spacecraft to mine[2] asteroids[3] for **precious** metals. One that the company hopes to find is platinum, a metal so rare on Earth that an ounce (about 28 grams) costs $1,600. Robots will have to travel millions of kilometers to locate and mine asteroids, and this **requires** technology that doesn't exist yet. This isn't stopping companies like Planetary Resources

1 If a vehicle is **unmanned**, there are no people in it.
2 When people **mine** for metals (like gold and silver), they dig deep holes in the ground to extract them.
3 An **asteroid** is an irregularly shaped rock, that orbits the sun mostly in a zone between Mars and Jupiter.

> ## "This is the beginning of the new space age."
> Mason Peck

45 Entrepreneur Elon Musk, the **founder** of SpaceX and other companies, is spending a large part of his **fortune** on his own space program. SpaceX, as mentioned earlier, is developing a new rocket that can transport supplies to the ISS. It will be 50 **capable** of carrying twice the cargo[4] of the U.S. government's space shuttle, Musk says, for about one-fifth the price. He wants to reduce costs by creating reusable rockets—in the same way that we reuse a plane after a flight. "Creating reusable 55 rockets will be **extremely** difficult, and most people think it's impossible, but I do not," Musk says. "If we threw away[5] airplanes after every flight, no one would fly."

For Musk, creating reusable rockets is part of 60 a much bigger plan: He wants to establish a human colony on Mars. NASA has had enormous success on Mars with unmanned spacecraft, but it has yet to launch a manned mission. Musk says SpaceX could put astronauts on Mars within 20 65 years, and then keep sending them for decades after that. "We can't send one little group to Mars," he says. "We have to take millions of people and lots of equipment to Mars to make it a self-**sustaining** civilization." It will be the 70 hardest thing that humanity has ever done, but Musk thinks his company can do it and he's eager to see it happen. "It's about making life multi-planetary," he says. "It's about getting out there and exploring the stars."

30 and others from trying, though. They are investing millions into research, hoping to create tools that will make space mining possible. "This is the beginning of the new space age," says Mason Peck, who works for NASA, the U.S. space organization. "The energy we see now—the economic motivation to go into 35 space—we haven't seen that before."

For centuries, economics has driven exploration. A thousand years ago, merchants risked the dangers of the Silk Road to reach the markets of China. In the 15th century, European ships traveled to new 40 worlds, searching less for knowledge than for gold and spices. "Historically, the driver has always been the search for resources," explains investor Peter Diamandis. If you want people to explore space, he says, create an economic incentive.

---

4 **Cargo** refers to the supplies a ship or plane carries.
5 If you **throw away** something, you get rid of it.

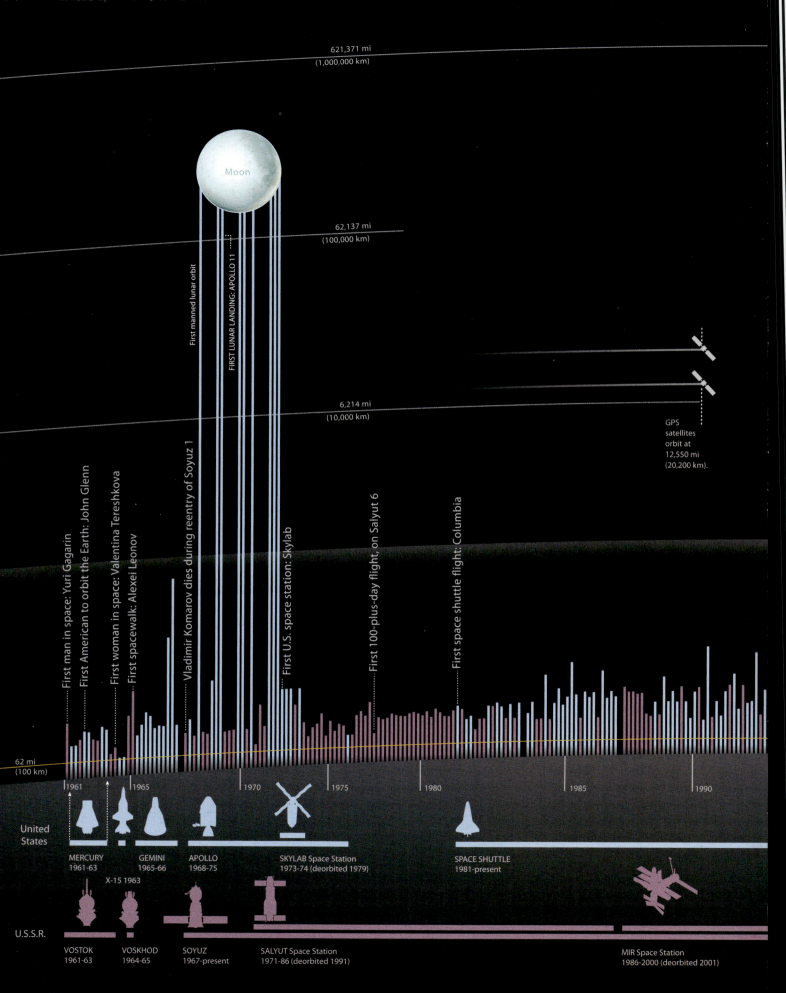

621,371 mi
(1,000,000 km)

Moon

62,137 mi
(100,000 km)

First manned lunar orbit

FIRST LUNAR LANDING: APOLLO 11

6,214 mi
(10,000 km)

GPS satellites orbit at 12,550 mi (20,200 km).

First man in space: Yuri Gagarin

First American to orbit the Earth: John Glenn

First woman in space: Valentina Tereshkova

First spacewalk: Alexei Leonov

Vladimir Komarov dies during reentry of Soyuz 1

First U.S. space station: Skylab

First 100-plus-day flight, on Salyut 6

First space shuttle flight: Columbia

62 mi
(100 km)

1961   1965   1970   1975   1980   1985   1990

United States

MERCURY 1961-63

X-15 1963

GEMINI 1965-66

APOLLO 1968-75

SKYLAB Space Station 1973-74 (deorbited 1979)

SPACE SHUTTLE 1981-present

U.S.S.R.

VOSTOK 1961-63

VOSKHOD 1964-65

SOYUZ 1967-present

SALYUT Space Station 1971-86 (deorbited 1991)

MIR Space Station 1986-2000 (deorbited 2001)

CHARTING THE MISSIONS

Since 1961, 500 men and women from some 40 countries have made 276 space missions, but few traveled beyond low Earth orbit. The next 50 years may bring another round of trips to the moon and make space travel a possibility for private citizens.

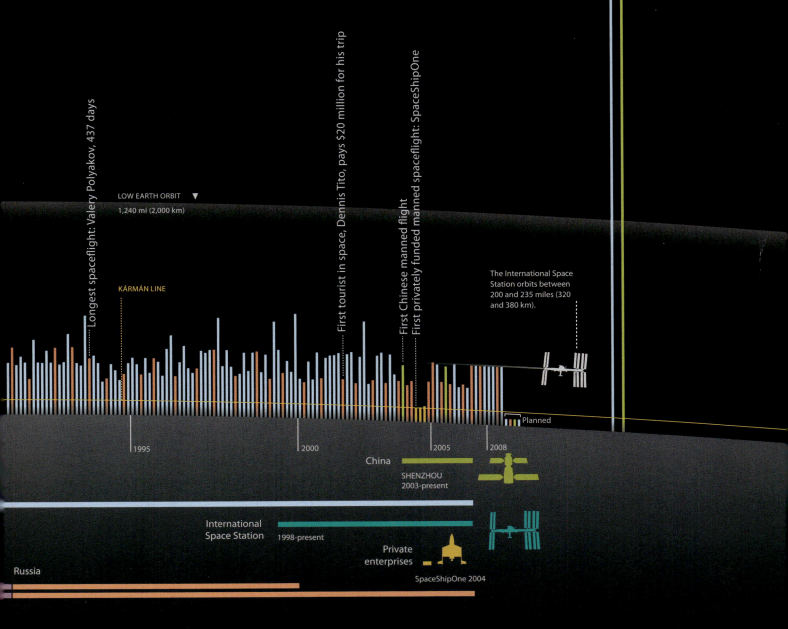

Mars

Moon

Longest spaceflight: Valery Polyakov, 437 days

LOW EARTH ORBIT ▼
1,240 mi (2,000 km)

KÁRMÁN LINE

First tourist in space, Dennis Tito, pays $20 million for his trip

First Chinese manned flight
First privately funded manned spaceflight: SpaceShipOne

The International Space Station orbits between 200 and 235 miles (320 and 380 km).

Planned

1995   2000   2005   2008

China

SHENZHOU
2003-present

International
Space Station   1998-present

Private
enterprises

SpaceShipOne 2004

Russia

Reading Comprehension

Multiple Choice. Choose the best answer for each question.

Detail **1.** Which statement about space exploration is NOT true?
   a. In 2012, a private company sent an unmanned rocket to the ISS.
   b. Humans have recently traveled more than 650 kilometers from Earth.
   c. There is newfound interest in manned and unmanned missions to space.
   d. More and more private companies are beginning to explore space.

Reference **2.** What does *one* refer to in line 22?
   a. one asteroid
   b. one metal
   c. one spacecraft
   d. one reason

Vocabulary **3.** What could the word *energy* be replaced with in line 33?
   a. fuel
   b. investments
   c. enthusiasm
   d. capacity

Main Idea **4.** What is the main idea of paragraph 4 (starting line 36)?
   a. Making money has always encouraged exploration, and space exploration is no different.
   b. It will take many more resources to convince people to travel to space.
   c. The development of space travel has been slow due to economic reasons.
   d. The search for knowledge is what should drive space exploration rather than economics.

Detail **5.** What does SpaceX want to do?
   a. build a space station that can replace the ISS
   b. get the government's approval to transport astronauts to the ISS
   c. partner with Planetary Resources to mine asteroids for platinum
   d. develop a reusable rocket that can take supplies to the ISS

Reference **6.** In line 72 what does *it* refer to?
   a. putting a few astronauts on Mars
   b. sending several unmanned spacecraft to Mars
   c. making a self-sustaining civilization on Mars
   d. transporting supplies to the ISS

Interpreting Charts **7.** When was the U.S. least active in space exploration?
   a. the early 60s to mid-60s
   b. the early 70s to mid-70s
   c. the late 70s to early 80s
   d. the late 80s

Critical Thinking

Interpreting: Why does Elon Musk mention airplanes (paragraph 5)? What point is he making?

Discussion: How likely do you think building a Mars space colony is? Would you be interested in going there?

Recognizing Appositives

Appositives are nouns or noun phrases that rename or identify another noun beside them by providing additional information. They can appear at the beginning, in the middle, or at the end of a sentence, and are set off by commas. For example:

A former navy pilot, Sunita Williams has performed seven spacewalks.

Sunita Williams, a former navy pilot, is now retired as an astronaut.

However, there are some structures that appear to be appositives but are not.

A thousand years ago, merchants risked the dangers of the Silk Road.

A. Analyzing. Check (✓) the sentences that contain appositives.

1. ☐ Neil Armstrong, the first man to walk on the moon, died in 2012.
2. ☐ A 722-kilogram space probe, Voyager 1 was launched in 1977 to study the solar system.
3. ☐ Several companies, hoping to take tourists into space, are taking reservations now.
4. ☐ In 2012, China became the third country to land a rover on the moon.

B. Applying. Rewrite each sentence with the correct appositive from the box. Then check your answers in the reading on pages 148–149.

> **the U.S. space organization**
> **the founder of SpaceX and other companies**
> **a private company based near Los Angeles**

1. Take, for example, SpaceX. (paragraph 2)

   _____

2. "This is the beginning of the new space age," says Mason Peck, who works for NASA. (paragraph 3)

   _____

   _____

3. Entrepreneur Elon Musk is spending a large part of his fortune on his own space program. (paragraph 5)

   _____

   _____

Vocabulary Practice

A. Completion. Complete the information below with words from the box. One word is extra.

backing	**capable**	**decades**	**extremely**
fortune	**precious**	**required**	**sustain**

Encouraged by new space technologies and the potential to generate riches, many companies, such as Deep Space Industries (DSI), say they will be **1.** _____ of mining asteroids in the coming **2.** _____.

There are thousands of near-Earth asteroids that contain **3.** _____ metals like gold and platinum. But other more basic elements such as water, nickel, and iron are also **4.** _____ in order to **5.** _____ a space colony and other ventures in space.

DSI's CEO, David Gump, says that obtaining resources from beyond Earth is essential for future space travel. This is because pushing through the Earth's atmosphere is **6.** _____ expensive. Some 90 percent of the weight lifted by a rocket sending a capsule to Mars is fuel. Space exploration would be much cheaper if some of the fuel could be picked up on the way. DSI is currently looking for financial **7.** _____ to make its dream a reality.

∧ Vesta, the third largest asteroid in the belt between Mars and Jupiter

B. Words in Context. Read the sentences and circle **T** (True) or **F** (False).

1. You might want to **replace** something that is old or broken.   T   F
2. A person who is suddenly awarded a **fortune** will probably be upset.   T   F
3. The **founder** of a company is the person who created it.   T   F
4. If something **sustains** you, it gives you something you need.   T   F
5. If something happened two **decades** ago, it happened 200 years ago.   T   F
6. If a course is **required** at college, it is not important to take it.   T   F

> **Word Partnership** Use **precious** with: (*n.*) precious **metal**, precious **stone**, precious **jewelry**, precious **cargo**, precious **moment**.

VIEWING Walking in Space

Before You Watch

A. True or False. What do you remember about spacewalking from the reading on pages 141–143? Read the sentences. Circle **T** for *true* or **F** for *false*.

1. American Edward White performed the first spacewalk.   **T**   **F**
2. Astronauts train for weightlessness in a tank of water.   **T**   **F**
3. Spacesuits have an internal heating and cooling system.   **T**   **F**
4. Spacewalks are normally performed alone in space.   **T**   **F**

∧ On February 12, 1984, astronaut Bruce McCandless ventured farther away from the safety of his ship than any previous astronaut.

While You Watch

A. Noticing. Check your answers to **A** on page 155. How many did you get right?

B. Sequence. Number the topics from 1 to 5 in the order they are discussed in the video.

_____ how spacesuits protect astronauts

_____ how spacewalkers train before going to space

_____ the first two people who performed spacewalks

_____ why spacewalking is difficult work

_____ tasks that spacewalkers perform

U.S. astronaut
Edward H. White II
carrying out external tasks
during an orbit of his spacecraft

"I'm coming back in . . . and it's the saddest moment of my life."

Edward H. White II, 1965

"I didn't feel like a giant. I felt very, very small."

Neil Armstrong, 1969

"The scenery was very beautiful. But I did not see the Great Wall [of China]."

Yang Liwei, 2003

"Just being there representing humanity was truly rewarding."

Sunita Williams, 2007

After You Watch

A. Discussion. Read the quotes above from four astronauts. Then discuss the questions below.

1. How would you describe each person's experience in space? Who do you think enjoyed it the most?

2. If you went to space, do you think you would have a similar reaction to any of the people?

10

ALL IN THE MIND

Frodo is the dominant male in his family of Gombe chimpanzees, living in Gombe Stream National Park, Tanzania.

Warm Up

Discuss these questions with a partner.

1. Do you think you have a good memory? What are your earliest memories?

2. How many different human emotions can you think of?

3. Which animals do you think are the most intelligent? Do you think that animals have the same emotions as humans?

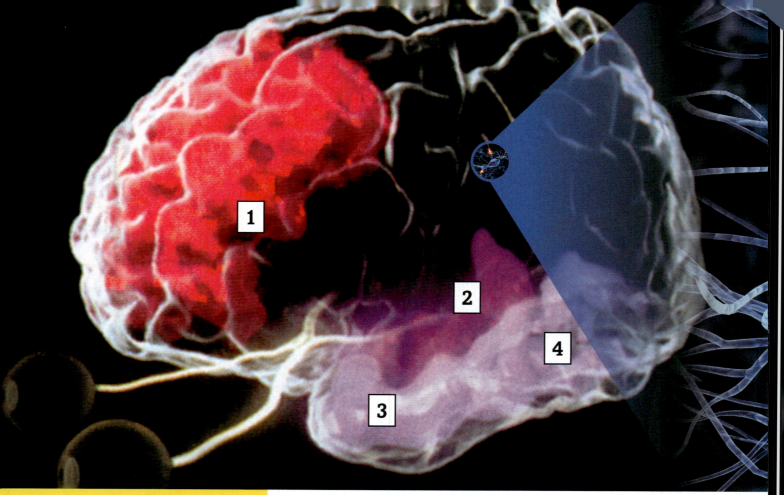

This brain scan shows four different parts of the brain. The prefrontal cortex [1] is key to an individual's **self-awareness**. The hippocampus [2] helps **recall** long-term memories. The amygdala [3] processes **emotional** memories. The temporal lobe [4] is associated with speech and **perception**.

Before You Read

A. Matching. Look at the image above and read the caption. Use the words in **bold** to complete the definitions.

1. If you have _____, it means you are conscious of your own identity.

2. If you are in a(n) _____ mental state, you display strong feelings.

3. If you are able to _____ something, you can remember it.

4. _____ is the recognition of things using your senses, especially sight.

B. Skim. Read the headings below and quickly skim the passage on pages 159–160. Which heading is most suitable for each break in the text? Label the headings **A–D**. Then read to check your answers.

_____ Who am I?   _____ How do I remember?

_____ Why do I have emotions?   _____ Can I control how I feel?

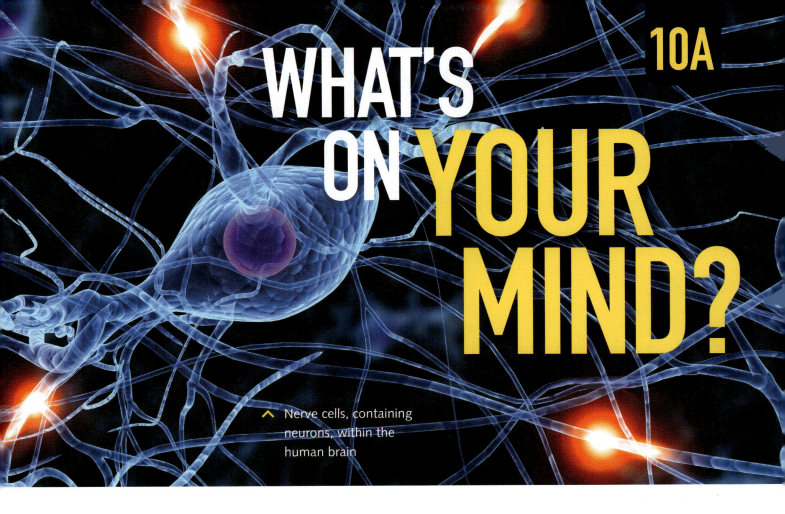

WHAT'S ON YOUR MIND?

∧ Nerve cells, containing neurons, within the human brain

1 The ancient Egyptians thought so little of the brain that when a king died, they removed the brain from his body and threw it away. The
5 Egyptians **presumed**, like many people before and after them, that consciousness—your mind and your thoughts—existed in the heart.

Today we know that the mind is a product of
10 the brain, but how exactly does this 1.5-kilo (three-pound) piece of flesh create a mind that allows you to think about yourself, experience happiness and anger, or remember events that happened 20 minutes or 20 years ago? This
15 isn't a new question. Today, however, powerful new techniques for **visualizing** the sources of thought, emotion, behavior, and memory are **transforming** the way we understand the brain and the mind it creates.

20 **A.** _____

Have you ever stopped and thought, "What's wrong with me today? I just don't feel like myself"? Perhaps you were more tired or worried than usual—but somehow, you
25 knew that something was different about you. This self-awareness—the ability to think about yourself and how you're feeling—is an important part of being human.

This part of your mind has its origins in the
30 prefrontal cortex—a region of your brain just behind your forehead that extends to about your ears. Before this area began to function (around age two), you didn't understand that you were a separate **entity** with your own
35 identity. In time, as this part of your brain developed, you became more aware of yourself and your thoughts and feelings.

B. _____

Perhaps one of the most important factors involved in shaping our identity is memory. What exactly is a memory? Most scientists define it as a stored pattern of connections between neurons[1] in the brain. Every feeling you remember, every thought you think, alters the connections within the **vast** network of brain cells, and memories are **reinforced**, weakened, or newly formed.

Most people's earliest memories reach back to about age three or so. Very few people recall anything before this time because the part of the brain that helps form long-term memories (the hippocampus) was not yet mature, or fully developed. This doesn't mean earlier memories don't exist in your mind, though. Some scientists believe highly emotional memories, especially those associated with intense fear, might be stored in another structure in the brain (the amygdala) that may be functional at birth. Though these memories are not accessible to the conscious mind, they might still influence the way we feel and behave, even into adulthood.

C. _____

But where do our emotions come from, and how do they shape the people we are and the way we perceive the world? Forty years ago, psychologist Paul Ekman demonstrated that facial expressions used to exhibit certain emotions are recognized by people everywhere. Ekman suggested that these emotions and their corresponding facial expressions evolved to help us deal quickly with situations that can affect our **welfare**.

Though humans may share certain emotions and recognize them in others, we don't all have the same emotional response to every situation. In fact, most emotional responses are learned and stored in our memories. The smell of freshly cut grass, for example, will generate happy feelings in someone who spent enjoyable childhood summers in the countryside, but not in someone who was forced to work long hours on a farm. Once an emotional association like this is made, it is very difficult to reverse it. "Emotion is the least **flexible** part of the brain," says Ekman. But we can learn to control our emotions by becoming consciously aware of their **underlying** causes and by not reacting automatically to things in our environment.

D. _____

But is it really possible to control our emotions? Researcher Richard Davidson has demonstrated that people who experience negative emotions display activity in their right prefrontal cortex. In those with a more positive **perspective**, the activity occurs in the left prefrontal cortex. Could we, Davidson wondered, control this activity and shift our mental state away from negative feelings toward a calmer state of mind?

To answer this question, Davidson worked with a group of volunteers in the United States. One group received eight weeks of training using different meditation[2] and relaxation techniques, while another group did not. By the end of the study, those who had meditated had accomplished their goal: They showed a clear shift in brain activity toward the left, "happier" frontal cortex.

For centuries, people have studied the brain, but it is only in recent years that we have really started to learn how it works. Nevertheless, there is still a long way to go before we understand our mind's many complexities.

---

1 A **neuron** is a cell that is part of the nervous system. Neurons send messages to and from the brain.

2 **Meditation** is the act of staying silent and calm for a period of time for spiritual or relaxation purposes.

Reading Comprehension

Multiple Choice. Choose the best answer for each question.

Gist **1.** What is this reading mainly about?
  a. how memory works
  b. how the mind works
  c. mind reading
  d. how our emotions are processed

Reference **2.** In line 11, *piece of flesh* refers to the _____.
  a. heart
  b. mind
  c. brain
  d. body

Detail **3.** Which of these statements is NOT true?
  a. Self-awareness develops around the age of two.
  b. The prefrontal cortex affects a person's emotions.
  c. The prefrontal cortex is located at the back of the brain.
  d. Memories depend on the connections between brain cells.

Vocabulary **4.** The word *corresponding* in line 71 is closest in meaning to _____.
  a. sending
  b. changing
  c. powerful
  d. related

Detail **5.** Why don't most people have memories of what happened before they were three years of age?
  a. The prefrontal cortex is not developed at this stage.
  b. Early memories disappear soon after they are formed.
  c. The part of the brain that forms memory is not fully developed at this stage.
  d. After the age of three, children tend to forget emotional memories.

Detail **6.** Where is the activity center for negative emotions?
  a. in the amygdala
  b. in the hippocampus
  c. in the left prefrontal cortex
  d. in the right prefrontal cortex

Detail **7.** According to researcher Richard Davidson, what helps people shift away from a negative state of mind?
  a. meditation and relaxation
  b. memory-retention techniques
  c. changing facial expressions
  d. being conscious of underlying emotions

Critical Thinking

Relating: What example of an emotional association does the author mention? Can you think of any examples from your own personal experience?

_____

Discussion: What do you think would be the benefits of a better understanding of the brain?

Identifying Definitions

Writers often define potentially unfamiliar vocabulary in a text. This can be done in a variety of ways. Sometimes, a definition follows words like *is/are*, *means*, *is defined as*, *is called*, and *is a type of*. It can also be set apart by parentheses **( )**, a dash or dashes **— —**, and a comma or commas **, ,**. A definition may be provided within a text or at the end of a text, for example as a footnote.

A. Completion. Complete the information with definitions from the box.

> **a. short-term**
> **b. sight, smell, sound, taste, and touch**
> **c. the outer layer of the brain**

Memory takes many different forms. The broadest categories of memory are _____ and long-term. Before we can make memories, we need to perceive and process information. The part of the brain responsible for information processing and sensations is the cerebral cortex—_____. Specialized parts of the cortex receive input from our senses (_____).

B. Completion. Look back at the reading passage on pages 159–160. Find and underline these words. Then write their definitions.

1. consciousness: _____

2. self-awareness: _____

3. prefrontal cortex: _____

4. memory: _____

5. neuron: _____

6. hippocampus: _____

7. mature: _____

Vocabulary Practice

A. Completion. Complete the information below using six words from the box.

entity	flexible	perspective	presume	reinforce
transform	underlying	vast	visualize	welfare

Memorizing information is an important skill for students. One technique for improving your memory is known as "mind-mapping." This method is the invention of a British researcher named Tony Buzan. From Buzan's
1. _____, no matter how weak you are as a student, the use of mind-mapping can **2.** _____ your mental ability and help you memorize a(n) **3.** _____ amount of information.

A mind map is similar to a word web (see page 179). It is a diagram of thoughts, starting from a single idea and spreading outward to new ideas, showing the connections between them. The **4.** _____ theory behind it is that by drawing the map, you are made to **5.** _____ the information clearly. Later, as you look at the mind map again and again, you
6. _____ your knowledge of the information and you memorize it.

B. Definitions. Use the remaining words in the box in **A** to complete the definitions.

1. A(n) _____ object or material can be bent easily without breaking.

2. If you _____ that something is true, you think it is true but are not certain.

3. A(n) _____ is something that exists separately from other things.

4. The _____ of a person or group is their health, comfort, and/or happiness.

> **Word Link** The suffix **-ible** means "able to be," e.g., *audible*, *flexible*, *possible*. The suffix **-ible** can often be changed to **-ibility** to form a noun, e.g., *flexibility*, *possibility*.

Before You Read

A. Discussion. Read the caption on the right. Do you think these animals can be called intelligent? How would you define "intelligence"?

B. Scan. Read the photo caption and skim the reading on the next page. You are going to read about animal intelligence. Quickly scan the reading to answer the questions below. Then read again to check your answers.

1. What animals are mentioned in the reading?

2. What kinds of "intelligence" does each animal display?

∧ **How smart are animals?** It's a question scientists are trying to answer. Birds, such as crows, have shown problem-solving skills and creativity by using tools such a metal wire to obtain food. Dolphins have demonstrated imitation and self-awareness by copying their trainers' movements. Sheep, and many other animals, demonstrate memory and emotions. They can recognize faces and also know if the person (or sheep) is happy or angry.

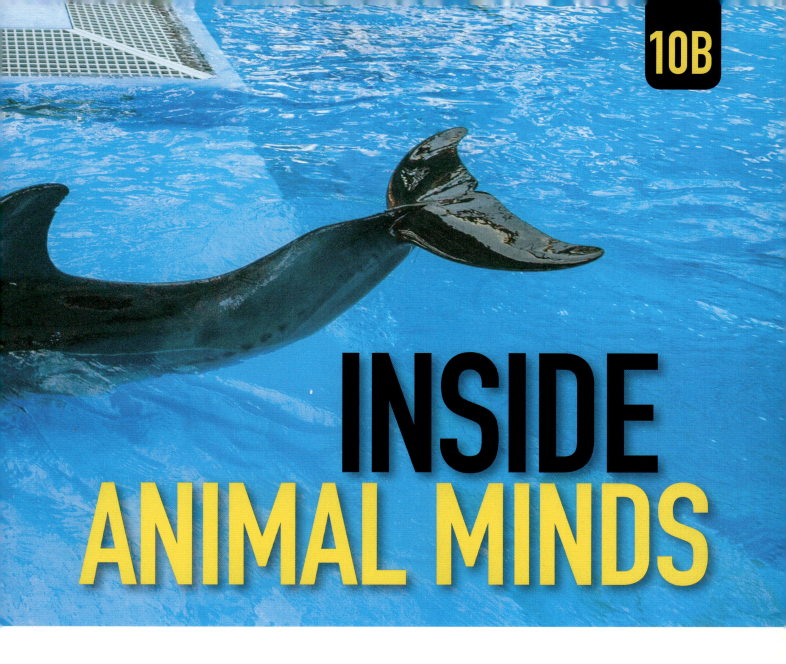

INSIDE ANIMAL MINDS

1   In 1977, Irene Pepperberg, a recent graduate of Harvard University, did something very unusual.

Pepperberg was interested in learning if animals could think, and the best way to do this, she reasoned, was to talk to them. To test her theory, she bought an
5   African grey parrot she named Alex and taught him to reproduce the sounds of the English language. "I thought if he learned to communicate, I could ask him questions about how he sees the world," she explains.

When Pepperberg began her research with Alex, very few scientists **acknowledged** that animals were capable of thought. The general belief was
10   that animals reacted to things in their environment but lacked the ability to think or feel. How, then, could a scientist demonstrate that animals might, in fact, possess intelligence? "That's why I started my studies with Alex," Pepperberg says.

Kanzi, a bonobo, understood the meaning of over 150 symbols.

Certain skills are considered key signs of higher mental abilities: a good memory, an understanding of symbols, self-awareness, understanding of others' motives, and creativity. Little by little, researchers have documented these abilities in other species. Sheep and elephants can recognize faces. Chimpanzees—who are genetically similar to humans—use a variety of **primitive** tools for eating, drinking, and hunting; they also laugh when pleased and spit[1] to show disgust with something. Octopuses in captivity[2] are known to amuse themselves by shooting water at laboratory staff. They may even exhibit basic emotions by changing color.

Alex the parrot was a surprisingly good talker. He learned how to use his voice to imitate almost 100 English words, including those for foods, colors, shapes, and numbers. Although imitation was once considered a simple skill, in recent years, cognitive scientists[3] have **revealed** that it's an extremely difficult ability. It requires the imitator to form a mental image of the other person's body and actions and then adjust his own body parts into the same position. It is a behavior that shows an awareness of one's self. Because Alex had **mastered** many English words, Pepperberg could ask him questions about a bird's basic understanding of the world. Alex could count, as well as describe shapes, colors, and sizes for Pepperberg; he even had an elementary understanding of the **abstract** concept of zero.

Many of Alex's cognitive skills, such as his ability to understand the concepts of same and different, are generally attributed only to higher mammals, particularly primates such as humans and apes. But parrots, like great apes (and humans), live a long time in complex societies.

---

1 If you **spit**, you force liquid out of your mouth.

2 An animal in **captivity** lives in a zoo, a cage, or other enclosed place.

3 A **cognitive scientist** studies the mind and its mental process.

Alex, an African grey parrot, had a large vocabulary and was able to answer questions about his understanding of the world.

And like primates, these birds must monitor the changing relationships within the group. This may explain Alex's ability to learn a human language. "When we take [parrots] into captivity, what they start to do is treat us as their flock,"[4] explains Pepperberg. Parrots learn to **pronounce** and use our words so they can become a part of our group.

Researchers in Germany and Austria have also been studying language ability in dogs. One named Betsy has shown that she is able to learn and remember words as quickly as a two-year-old child. She has an **extraordinary** vocabulary of over 340 words (and counting), knows at least 15 people by name, and can link photographs with the real objects they represent. Like Alex, she's pretty smart. This is the larger lesson of animal cognition research: It **humbles** us. We are not alone in our ability to invent, communicate, demonstrate emotions, or think about ourselves. Still, humans remain the creative species. No other animal has built cities, created music, or made a computer. In fact, a number of critics **dismiss** animals' ability to use tools or understand human language. They believe animals are just **simulating** human behavior.

Yet, many researchers say that creativity and language in animals, like other forms of intelligence, have evolved. "People were surprised to discover that chimpanzees make tools," says Alex Kacelnik, an animal researcher at Oxford University. "But people also thought, 'Well, they share our ancestry—of course they're smart.' Now we're finding these kinds of behaviors in some species of birds. But we don't have a recently shared ancestry with birds. It means," Kacelnik continues, "that evolution can invent similar forms of advanced intelligence more than once—that it's not something reserved only for primates or mammals."

4 A **flock** of birds is a group of birds.

Reading Comprehension

Multiple Choice. Choose the best answer for each question.

Gist
1. What is this reading mainly about?
   a. ways of teaching animals to become more intelligent
   b. research that shows intelligence is not limited to humans
   c. how animals can communicate with humans
   d. how human and animal intelligence are different

Detail
2. Which of the following is NOT mentioned in the passage?
   a. how an octopus displays basic emotions
   b. ways in which elephants communicate with each other
   c. how birds and chimps evolved tool-making abilities
   d. the language ability of dogs

Detail
3. What could Alex do that showed self-awareness?
   a. count
   b. learn vocabulary
   c. copy human sounds
   d. understand the concept of zero

Reference
4. In line 39, *It* refers to _____.
   a. counting
   b. talking
   c. imitating
   d. asking questions

Detail
5. What do parrots and primates have in common?
   a. They both live a long time in complex societies.
   b. They both learn to use tools while in captivity.
   c. They both teach new human words to their young.
   d. Neither likes to participate in or be part of a group.

Vocabulary
6. In line 67, the word *link* could be replaced with _____.
   a. match
   b. take
   c. count
   d. view

Inference
7. Which statement would Alex Kacelnik probably agree with?
   a. Only humans and primates are capable of thought.
   b. Birds share a common ancestry with humans.
   c. Some birds are more intelligent than humans.
   d. We can find intelligence in species we don't normally consider intelligent.

Critical Thinking

Evaluating: Do you think all of the animals discussed in the reading can be called "intelligent"? Which would you say is the most intelligent? Why?

Discussion: Can you think of other examples of animal intelligence that are not mentioned in the reading?

Identifying Lexical Cohesion

Lexical cohesion is a feature of cohesive writing. Writers often use different words to avoid repetition and to add variety to a text. One way to achieve this is to use synonyms. Sometimes, instead of two words being exact synonyms, one word may be a more specific (or a more general) part of, or an example of, another word. Look at the following examples:

The aroma in the kitchen got my attention. The smell of cookies took me back to my childhood. (Here, *aroma* and *smell* refer to the same thing.)

I bought flour, sugar, and cocoa. After I got the ingredients home, I realized I had no vanilla. (Here, flour, sugar, cocoa, and vanilla are specific examples of ingredients.)

A. Classification. These words are from the reading passage on page 165–167. Find pairs of synonyms and write them below.

ability	action	basic	behavior
communicate	create	elementary	exhibit
imitate	invent	reason	reproduce
show	skill	talk	think

1. _____ = _____

2. _____ = _____

3. _____ = _____

4. _____ = _____

5. _____ = _____

6. _____ = _____

7. _____ = _____

8. _____ = _____

B. Analyzing. In each extract below, circle the general term once and double-underline any specific part or examples of the word.

1. . . . researchers have documented these abilities in other species. Sheep and elephants can recognize faces. (lines 18–20)

2. . . . particularly primates such as humans and apes. (lines 50–51)

3. . . . humans remain the creative species. (line 73)

4. . . . researchers say that creativity and language in animals, like other forms of intelligence, have evolved. (lines 79–81)

Vocabulary Practice

A. Completion. Complete the paragraph with words from the box. Two words are extra.

abstract	acknowledging	dismiss	extraordinarily
mastered	revealed	primitive	pronounce

Research in the Fongoli region of Senegal has **1.** _____ that chimpanzees seem to have **2.** _____ the art of basic tool-making. Furthermore, a chimp was observed sharpening a stick with her teeth before using it as a(n) **3.** _____ tool for killing a bush baby.[1]

Although few people completely **4.** _____ the findings, some researchers question their significance. Primatologist Craig Stanford, for example, while **5.** _____ that the behavior is fascinating, finds that the research findings are only important enough to be ". . . a short note in a journal." However, researcher Jill Pruetz claims that the discovery is remarkable, as it shows that chimp behavior can be **6.** _____ humanlike.

B. Definitions. Complete the sentences with words from the box. Two words are extra.

abstract	acknowledge	dismiss	extraordinary
humble	master	pronounce	simulate

1. To _____ something means to become skilled in the use of it.

2. If you _____ an action or a feeling, you copy it or pretend to do it.

3. To _____ a word means to say it using particular sounds.

4. A(n) _____ person is not proud, and does not believe he or she is better than other people.

5. If you _____ a fact or situation, you accept or admit that it is true.

6. A(n) _____ idea or way of thinking is based on general ideas rather than on real things and events.

Senegal

^ [1] A **bush baby** is a small animal with large eyes that lives in Africa.

Thesaurus
master Also look up: (*n.*) *owner, artist, expert, professional*; (*v.*) *learn, study, understand*

VIEWING Chimp Memory

Before You Watch

A. Work in a Group. Do you think you have a good memory? Try this memory task.

Look at these numbers for 30 seconds. Then cover them and try to write them in the same place in the chart to the right. Who did the best?

5	9	0	3
2	1	7	6
4	6	2	8
2	0	9	1

B. Do you think chimps would be able to do this activity? Why or why not?

While You Watch

A. Completion. Circle the correct word or phrase to complete each caption.

Dr. Matsuzawa taught chimps to (**recognize / draw the shapes of**) numbers.

In the test, the numbers were later replaced with (**white squares / other numbers**).

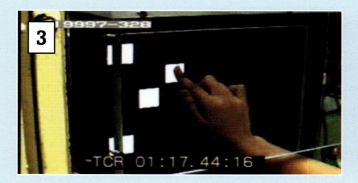

When the speed was increased, the humans were (**more / less**) accurate.

Photographic memory has been shown to be present in chimps and (**some human children / most adult humans**).

A. Main Idea. Check (✓) the statement(s) that best summarizes the video.

  ☐ Young chimps have been taught to use a computer.

  ☐ Young chimps do better at some memory tests than humans.

  ☐ Young chimps can easily be taught how to count to 10.

B. Discussion. Discuss these questions with a partner.

1. What might be some other ways we could learn about chimpanzee intelligence?
2. Look back at your answers to question 3 on page 157. Have your opinions changed after completing this unit?

11

ART AND LIFE

National Portrait Gallery,
Washington, D.C., U.S.A.

Warm Up

Discuss these questions with a partner.

1. Who are some of your favorite artists? Why do you like them?

2. What are some popular works of art in your country? Why are they popular?

3. Do you think that colors affect people's emotions? How?

173

Before You Read

A. **Scan.** Look quickly at the reading on pages 175–177. Which colors are discussed in the passage? Note them in the chart. What feelings, beliefs, etc., do you associate with each color? Note them in the second column.

B. Read the passage. Add information you learn in the third column.

Color	Things I associate with this color	Things I learned about this color
1.		
2.		
3.		

THE POWER OF COLOR

SOUTH AFRIC.

1   Thinkers, artists, and scientists have long debated
    the nature of color: What are its origins, and how
    does it affect us?

∧ Colorful lights and
advertising at night
on Nanjing Road,
Shanghai, China

Early humans watched their fires blacken the ceilings of the caves
5   where they lived. They saw blue and red in the sky and brown
    and green on the ground. In time, people began to understand
    that color not only made the world more beautiful, it was also
    able to **convey** emotion and symbolize power. Using colors they
    extracted from insects, plants, and minerals, primitive humans
10 copied animals, painting their bodies to signal **aggression**
    toward an enemy or to attract a mate.

Over the centuries, the sources of colors such as blue, purple,
and red were carefully guarded and were often worth as much
as gold. In the 19th century, a young chemistry student became
15 the first to manufacture a synthetic[1] dye,[2] and suddenly the world
became a much more colorful place. By the 20th century, as
scientists discovered the psychological effects of colors, everyone
from advertisers to educators found ways to make use of color to
influence our feelings and behavior.

1 **Synthetic** products are
made from chemicals, not
natural materials.

2 A **dye** is a substance that
is mixed into a liquid and
used to change the color
of something, such as
cloth or hair.

Red

20

Red, the color of human blood, has traditionally symbolized intensity, fire, love, and anger. In Eastern cultures, it also represents luck, wealth, and success. In

25 humans, the color red can send different messages. Some people redden, for example, when they are angry or embarrassed, sending a clear signal to others about how they are feeling. British anthropologists Russell

30 Hill and Robert Barton of the University of Durham found that when opponents in a game are equally matched, the team dressed in red is more likely to win. Why? According to Barton, "red seems to be the color, across

35 species, that signals dominance"[3]—giving those dressed in red an advantage in sporting events. In many animal species (including humans), contact with this **bold** color causes the heart rate to accelerate. However, one

40 of red's lighter shades, pink, can have the opposite effect on people. Men in prisons[4] are reported to be more **passive** when the walls are painted a specific shade of pink.

Humans have also used the color red in
45 everything from politics to advertising. Many food products in the U.S., for example, are **packaged** in red containers. Why? The color makes the product look as if it is advancing toward a shopper.

Yellow

50

Yellow, the color we most often associate with sunshine, is found throughout nature and the man-made world as a color that commands attention; indeed, it is one of the

55 easiest colors to see. This highly visible shade is found on everything from school buses to traffic signs and pens used to highlight important information in a text. The color is also used to **caution** people. Soccer players,

60 for example, are shown yellow as a reminder to behave. It can be used as a stimulant as

∧ Colorful spotlights illuminate the limestone formations at Reed Flute Cave, Guilin, China.

well: In a number of studies, yellow has been found to help children focus on their work and do better in school.

Blue

65

Blue, the color of sky and sea, has long been associated in many cultures with water, holy or religious objects, and protection against evil.[5] Over the years, darker shades of the color

---

3 If a person is **dominant**, he or she has power and influence over others.

4 A **prison** is a building where criminals are kept as punishment.

5 **Evil** is a powerful force that some people believe exists, and which causes bad things to happen.

have also come to represent calm, stability, and power. Dark blue, for example, is the color of the business suit or police uniform; it tells others, "I am in control" or "You can trust me." In other cultures, blue has been associated with sadness. It's common in English, for example, when feeling sad or **depressed**, to talk about "feeling blue," while in Iran, blue is the color of mourning, worn when a person dies.

Like pink, blue has a **neutral**, calming effect on people. Rooms painted blue help people relax or sleep. (Sleeping pills are often colored blue to suggest exactly this idea.) The color also seems to **inhibit** hunger. Blue food is rarely seen in nature, and when it is, such food is usually no longer healthy to consume (with the exception of certain fruits like blueberries). Thus, eating off blue plates may reduce one's hunger. So if you're planning to lose weight, try adding a blue light to your refrigerator—it will make the food inside look less appetizing. It's just one more example of the power that color can hold over us.

Reading Comprehension

Multiple Choice. Choose the best answer for each question.

Gist

1. What is this reading mainly about?
   a. how color influences our lives
   b. the various sources for extracting color
   c. how views about color have changed
   d. how certain colors can have a calming effect

Detail

2. The first non-natural colors were produced _____.
   a. many centuries ago
   b. in the 19th century
   c. in the 20th century
   d. only recently

Detail

3. According to the passage, which color can give a sports team a competitive advantage?
   a. black
   b. yellow
   c. blue
   d. red

Vocabulary

4. In line 39, what does the word *accelerate* mean?
   a. go slower
   b. go faster
   c. become uneven
   d. become louder

Detail

5. Which color has been used to help children study better?
   a. red
   b. yellow
   c. blue
   d. pink

Reference

6. In line 83, *this idea* refers to _____.
   a. inhibiting hunger
   b. blue food
   c. relaxation
   d. painting rooms

Detail

7. According to the passage, what do the colors pink and blue have in common?
   a. They both have a calming effect.
   b. They both make people less hungry.
   c. They both express sadness.
   d. They both represent power.

Critical Thinking

Evaluating: What evidence does the author provide for the "power that color can hold over us"? Do you agree with the author that color has a powerful effect on people?

Discussion: What do colors signify in your culture? Think about the colors used for political parties, police uniforms, advertising, traffic signs, etc.

Creating a Word Web

A word web is a diagram that helps you visualize the important ideas of a text. It is used to represent relationships that are connected to a central and more prominent idea. The main topic of the text is typically placed in the center of the diagram. Important subtopics are clustered around the main topic. The specific details are then clustered around the subtopics, and so on.

A. Classification. What do you remember about the passage, "The Power of Color"? Write one word for each of the blanks in the word web.

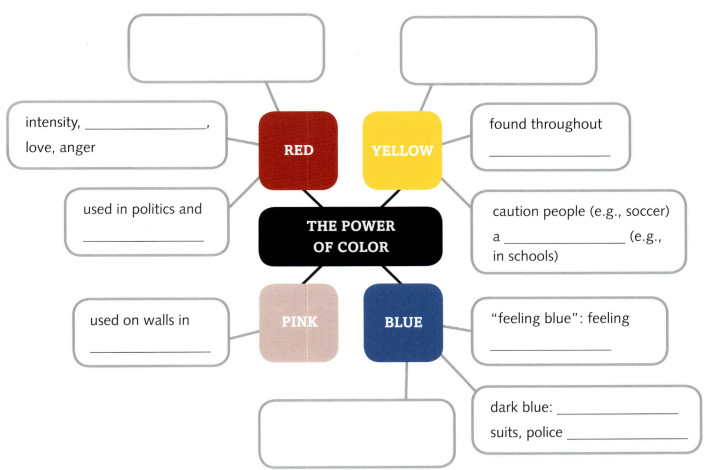

intensity, _____, love, anger

RED

YELLOW

found throughout _____

used in politics and _____

THE POWER OF COLOR

caution people (e.g., soccer) a _____ (e.g., in schools)

used on walls in _____

PINK

BLUE

"feeling blue": feeling _____

dark blue: _____ suits, police _____

B. Look back at the passage on pages 175–177 to check your answers in **A**. Use information from the reading to add other details to the blank boxes in the word web.

A. Completion. Complete the information with the correct form of words from the box. One word is extra.

> **bold   caution   depressed   extract   inhibition   passive**

One of the biggest celebrations of the year in India is *Holi*, also known as "The Festival of Colors." Held annually in late February or early March, *Holi* is celebrated by lighting bonfires and throwing colored powder and water on friends and family.

Days before the start of the festival, the markets are filled with
1. _____ colors of all shades, from bright red to the deepest blue. Many families create their own colors at home, often using dyes **2.** _____ from flowers. On the day of the festival, children and adults alike put aside their
3. _____ and enjoy throwing colored paint at each other.

The *Holi* festival is a popular event with both locals and visitors. However, a note of **4.** _____: Even if you plan only to be a(n) **5.** _____ onlooker, don't wear your best clothes. It's likely they will be covered with paint by the time you return home!

∧ Children celebrating the Hindu festival of *Holi* in India

B. Definitions. Complete the sentences with the correct form of words from the box. One word is extra.

> **aggressive   bold   convey   depressed   neutral   package**

1. If you are _____ about something, you feel neither strongly for, nor against, it.

2. To _____ information or feelings is to make them known or understood.

3. If you are _____, you are sad and feel that you cannot enjoy anything.

4. A(n) _____ is a small bag, box, or envelope in which something is stored or sold.

5. A(n) _____ person or animal behaves angrily or violently toward others.

> **Usage** We stress the second syllable of the verb *extract*, but the first syllable of the noun, **ex**tract. Other examples are con**trast** (*v.*) vs. **con**trast (*n.*); re**cord** (*v.*) vs. **rec**ord (*n.*); pro**duce** (*v.*) vs. **prod**uce (*n.*); trans**fer** (*v.*) vs. **trans**fer (*n.*).

VAN GOGH's WORLD

Before You Read

A. Quiz. How much do you know about the famous artist Vincent van Gogh? Circle your answers.

1. What was van Gogh's nationality?
   a. Belgian   b. Dutch

2. In what year was van Gogh born?
   a. 1853   b. 1903

3. At what age did van Gogh decide to be a painter?
   a. 6   b. 26

4. What kind of flower is van Gogh famous for painting?
   a. red roses   b. yellow sunflowers

B. Scan. Scan the first two paragraphs on page 182 to check your answers. Then read the rest of the passage.

1 STARRY NIGHTS AND SUNFLOWERS, self-portraits and café settings—all painted in bold, intense colors. Today, people around the world immediately recognize these as the work of Vincent van Gogh, the Dutch painter. Probably no

5 other artist, at any time in any culture, has achieved such popularity. But who was this man exactly, and why, even today, do his art and life have such an ability to move us?

An Artist Is Born

Vincent van Gogh was born on March 30, 1853, in a small

10 village in southern Holland. As a child, he was serious and **sensitive**. He loved to draw, and his work showed talent, but no one encouraged him to become an artist. Instead, his father thought he should take a "**sensible**" job—something like a salesclerk or carpenter. As a young adult, he **wandered**

15 from job to job with little success and very little money, becoming more depressed with each failure. In March 1880, however, just before his 27th birthday, something changed inside van Gogh. He realized that he was meant to be a painter, and he began to study art in Brussels, receiving a

20 **subsidy** from his brother Theo, which helped him to live.

Discovering Color

In 1886, van Gogh moved to Paris, hoping to learn more about color techniques being used by Impressionist artists there. Instead of grays and browns, his work began to

25 emphasize blue and red, and then yellow and orange. Soon he began to see life differently: Go slow. Stop thinking. Look around. You'll see something beautiful if you open yourself. These were the principles that guided his art. With his **innovative** color combinations, van Gogh wanted to show

30 his viewers how to better **appreciate** a flower, the night sky, or a person's face.

Descent into Madness

Few who lived in van Gogh's time appreciated his work, however. Many laughed when they saw his paintings, which

35 hurt the sensitive artist terribly. In February 1888, he moved away from Paris to Arles, a town in southern France. Often he could not eat or sleep, and stayed up into the early morning hours painting. Days passed, and he spoke to no one. Following an argument with fellow artist Paul Gauguin,

40 van Gogh took a razor and cut off his own earlobe.[1]

---

1 Your **earlobe** is the soft part at the bottom of your ear.

Starry Night, June 1889

Few who lived in van Gogh's time appreciated his work . . .

He never explained why, but by now, many were convinced that van Gogh was crazy, and indeed, his mental health started to decline. He began to have attacks during which he would hear strange sounds and think people were trying to hurt him. In the spring of 1889, he was sent to a mental hospital in St. Rémy, a town near Arles.

What exactly was van Gogh suffering from? No one knows for sure, but some now think it may have been a form of manic depression.[2] Whatever his condition, van Gogh's illness both inhibited and inspired his creativity. When his attacks came, he could not paint. But during his periods of calm, he was able to complete more than a hundred masterpieces, including the **classic** *Starry Night*. "Working on my pictures," he wrote, "is almost a necessity for my **recovery**."

Final Days

Following his release from the hospital in May 1890, van Gogh took a room in a town just north of Paris. For the 70 days that he lived there, he produced, on average, a painting a day. Until his death, however, he was unable to sell a single one; today, those paintings would be worth more than a billion U.S. dollars.

It was at this time that van Gogh either borrowed or stole a gun. On the afternoon of July 27, 1890, he went out to the country and shot himself in the stomach. Two days later, Vincent van Gogh died at age 37. What caused him to take his own life—his lack of financial success, mental illness, his loneliness?

Van Gogh's Legacy[3]

Over a century after his death, van Gogh still remains extremely popular. His story— of a man who **resisted** materialism[4] and **greed**, who was alone and unappreciated— gives people something they need. We find pieces of ourselves in him. This may also explain the high prices paid for van Gogh's work. His *Portrait of Dr. Gachet* sold in 1990 for more than $80 million to a Japanese businessman, breaking the world record for art pieces. Many of his other works have also sold for millions. Of course, people are buying great art when they purchase one of van Gogh's paintings. But they are also buying a piece of his story, which, like his work, will live on forever.

---

2 **Manic depression**, or bipolar disorder, is a medical condition in which someone sometimes feels excited and confident and at other times very depressed.

3 A **legacy** is something that comes from someone in the past.

4 **Materialism** is attaching a lot of importance to money and having a lot of things.

The Church in Auvers (1890) > was one of Vincent van Gogh's final paintings.

Reading Comprehension

Multiple Choice. Choose the best answer for each question.

Detail

1. Which statement is NOT true about van Gogh's youth?
   a. He grew up in Holland.
   b. He was born in a small village.
   c. His parents encouraged his artistic talent.
   d. He tried several jobs but was unsuccessful.

Purpose

2. What is the purpose of paragraph 2 (starting line 11)?
   a. to advise when van Gogh was born
   b. to describe how van Gogh became a painter
   c. to show that van Gogh was a troubled man
   d. to show how van Gogh survived on his own

Main Idea

3. What is the main idea in paragraph 3 (starting line 22)?
   a. Van Gogh was unhappy working with painters in Holland.
   b. Van Gogh's move to Paris changed his attitude toward art.
   c. Van Gogh was less successful than other Impressionist painters.
   d. Van Gogh's paintings of flowers were very popular in Paris.

Paraphrase

4. Which of the following is closest in meaning to *Working on my pictures is almost a necessity for my recovery*. (lines 56–58)?
   a. I need to paint in order to heal myself.
   b. I need to get better so that I can paint again.
   c. I will improve only if I stop painting.
   d. I will paint only after I feel better.

Vocabulary

5. In line 61, the word *took* is closest in meaning to _____.
   a. left
   b. moved into
   c. stole from
   d. sold

Detail

6. What is NOT suggested as a possible motive for van Gogh's suicide?
   a. lack of financial success
   b. mental illness
   c. his parents' lack of support
   d. loneliness

Cohesion

7. The following sentence would best be placed at the end of which paragraph? *The question, like so many others in van Gogh's life, remains unanswered.*
   a. 1 (starting line 1)
   b. 2 (starting line 9)
   c. 7 (starting line 60)
   d. 8 (starting line 67)

Critical Thinking

Relating: The author says that we can find pieces of ourselves in van Gogh. Do you agree? In what way can you relate to van Gogh?

_____

Discussion: Why do you think paintings by artists like van Gogh are so valuable today? What do you think motivates people to spend tens of millions of dollars for a painting?

Reading Skill

Sequencing Information

When you sequence information, you put things in the order in which they occur. This can help you understand how key events in a text relate to each other, such as cause and effect relationships. It is especially useful to sequence information from stories or biographical texts.

A. Sequencing. Number the events in van Gogh's life in the order in which they occurred (**1–6**).

_____ shows artistic talent in his hometown Zundert, but receives little encouragement

_____ relocates to Brussels to learn the skills needed to be an artist

_____ produces a painting a day for just over two months in Auvers, near Paris

_____ studies the techniques of Impressionist painters in Paris and changes his use of colors

_____ spends hours painting in the fields of Arles; argues with fellow painter Paul Gauguin

_____ recovers from depression in a hospital in St. Rémy; paints *Starry Night*

B. Mapping. Use information from the reading to sketch the route van Gogh took during his life, from his birthplace to the place where he died.

A. Completion. Complete the information with the correct form of words from the box. One word is extra.

appreciate classic innovative resist subsidize wander

Many Impressionist painters greatly admired the woodblock[1] prints of Japanese artists such as Hokusai and Hiroshige. The techniques of these woodblock artists, such as the use of strong black lines, were new, exciting, and **1.** _____. However, other Western artists **2.** _____ this movement and advocated a return to a more traditional, **3.** _____ view of art and the use of older techniques.

Van Gogh especially **4.** _____ the work of Japanese woodblock artists. During the time he spent **5.** _____ in the fields near Arles, he felt a close relationship with Japanese art and culture, and even shaved his head to "look like a Japanese monk."

---

1 **Woodblock** printing involves carving an image into a piece of wood, which is then inked and stamped onto a page.

∧ In 1887, van Gogh created *Bridge in the Rain*, a version of this woodcut by Hiroshige.

B. Words in Context. Complete each sentence with the correct answer.

1. If you describe someone as **greedy**, you mean they want to have _____ of something than they need.
   a. more
   b. less

2. When you **recover** from an illness or injury, you become _____.
   a. well again
   b. sicker

3. If a decision is **sensible**, it usually means it is based on _____.
   a. emotion
   b. reason

4. If you are **sensitive** to other people's needs or feelings, you _____.
   a. show understanding of them
   b. are not aware of them

5. If a government, an authority, or a person **subsidizes** something, they _____ of it.
   a. pay part of the cost
   b. take ownership

Word Link The word root **sen(s)** means "feeling or being aware," e.g., *sensation, sensitive, senseless, sensible, sensory, resent, consent.*

VIEWING Urban Art

A. Discussion. Look at the image and caption. How would you describe this art? Why do you think it was created?

Graffiti on the wall of a building on New York's Lower East Side

B. Completion. Read the information below and use the correct form of the words in **bold** to complete the sentences.

Urban art—sometimes referred to as "street art"—is a style of art that relates to cities and city life. One distinctive form of urban art is **graffiti** art. Art **gallery** owner Chris Murray believes that graffiti art is an important step in the evolution of pop art—an art style that **emerged** in the mid-20th century. Pop art borrows heavily from popular mass culture, such as comic books and advertising, and has brought a new **dimension** to modern art.

1. _____ means "belonging to or relating to a city or town."

2. A(n) _____ is a place where people go to look at works of art.

3. When an organization or a movement _____, it comes into existence.

4. A(n) _____ of something is a particular aspect of it.

5. _____ is words or pictures that are written or drawn in public places.

While You Watch

A. Completion. Complete these quotes with the missing words.

Nick Posada, Graffiti Artist:

"This is what happens when nobody _____ any type of work that someone spent their _____ and their time on."

Chris Murray, Govinda Gallery:

"Graffiti art has certainly brought to _____ art a whole new _____."

Don Kimes, American University:

"It's about sort of taking what it is that you come from, what you emerge from, what's authentic for you, and _____ it to the _____ of its envelope."

B. True or False. Mark the statements **T** (True) or **F** (False).

1. The Wall of Fame is a gallery in Washington, D.C.   **T**   **F**
2. Nick Posada feels there are rules to be followed in the world of graffiti.   **T**   **F**
3. Posada says you should use colors that complement one another.   **T**   **F**
4. Young people and collectors of pop art are buying graffiti art.   **T**   **F**

After You Watch

A. Paraphrasing. Look at the paraphrases below. Choose the one that best paraphrases the quotes in part **A** above.

1. Nick Posada
   a. This is what happens when people think art is not worth respecting and so don't spend time appreciating it.
   b. This is what happens when people do not respect the time and effort an individual puts into their art.

2. Chris Murray
   a. The new aspects of graffiti are what make this art popular.
   b. Graffiti has shown people a new form and aspect of art.

3. Don Kimes
   a. Artists must draw from their experiences and background and use that as an inspiration to produce art.
   b. Artists must always push themselves to work harder so that they can improve themselves and their art.

12

MEDICAL
CHALLENGES

Scientists handle biohazardous samples in the laboratory

Warm Up

Discuss these questions with a partner.

1. What are some major health concerns for people in your country?

2. What do you think will be some important medical advances in the next 10 years? 100 years?

3. What are some health issues that have been in the news recently? What do you know about them?

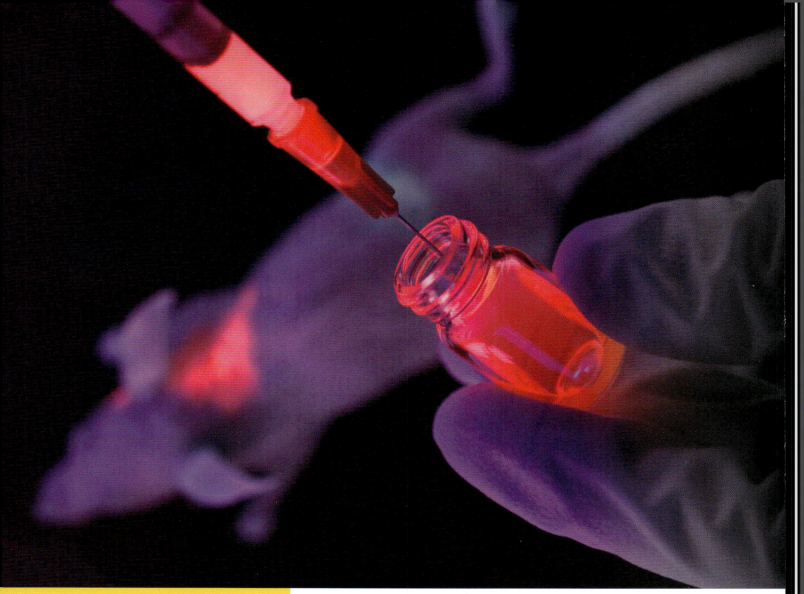

Before You Read

A. Discussion. Look at the photo and caption on this page, and discuss the questions below.

1. What are the most serious health problems facing the world today?

2. What major advances in medicine have there been in the past two decades?

B. Predict. Read the first paragraph on page 193. What is the reading mainly about? Circle **a**, **b**, or **c**. Then read the passage to check your answer.

a. a new technology involving extremely small particles

b. a new technology taken from animals

c. a new technology that can prevent the spread of killer viruses

∧ Nanoparticles of cadmium selenide that glow under ultraviolet light are injected into a healthy mouse. These particles are able to enter cancerous tumors, enabling surgeons to remove the sick cells without harming the healthy ones.

A CURE FOR CANCER?

1 In the 1966 science-fiction film *Fantastic Voyage*, a team of scientists and doctors are shrunk and injected into the body of an
5 injured man to save his life. The tiny crew travels through the body's dangerous environment to locate and repair the damaged part of the man's body. Eventually,
10 the group manages to complete their task and the man awakens, fully cured.

Such an idea, while fun, sounds extraordinary to many. But what if it were possible to cure a
15 disease like cancer using tiny particles injected into a person—particles that would not only find the cancer, but also destroy it without harming anything else in the body? Although it may seem like science fiction, tools like this are now being
20 developed and may, in fact, become common in the near future—thanks to research currently being done in the field of nanotechnology.

The main thing to know about nanotechnology is that it's small—really small. The prefix *nano*
25 (meaning "dwarf"[1] in Greek) refers to a nanometer, which is one-billionth of a meter. How small is that exactly?

---

1 **Dwarf** is used to describe varieties of plants or animals that are smaller than the usual size.

Perhaps that old movie, *Fantastic Voyage,* isn't so hard to believe after all.

A comma on a page of a book or magazine, for instance, may be more than half a million nanometers wide. Understanding the "science of small" may eventually allow doctors to diagnose[2] and cure illnesses like heart disease and cancer early, before they can do **extensive** damage to the body.

Researcher Ted Sargent, a leader in the field of nanotechnology, describes how using quantum dots[3]—particles that are a few nanometers in size—will help diagnose a disease. The particles, Sargent explains, shine brightly when exposed to UV light and can be **inserted** into the body. They can also be programmed to **bond** only to a certain type of cell—a particular cancer cell, for example. Doctors can then use a camera and look for the colored particles, which will help them determine where cancer cells are growing in a person's body.

Using this technology, it will be possible to detect cancer at a stage when there are perhaps only a thousand bad cells. Compare this to what happens today: Doctors can diagnose cancer only after the dangerous cells have **multiplied** into the millions and developed into a tumor. One of the advantages of detecting and treating cancer at an early stage is that the cells are less likely to become resistant to drug treatment. In later stages, cancer cells often change and adapt to certain drugs so rapidly that many medicines become ineffective.

Once a certain type of cancer is detected, nanotechnology will also **radically** improve the way it is treated. Right now, most cancer treatments kill not only the cancerous cells but the healthy ones as well, causing a number of side effects in people, such as hair loss, nausea,[4] and intense pain. Nanoparticles, on the other hand, will allow doctors to attack cancerous tumors without disturbing healthy cells. The goal will be to deliver cancer-killing drugs, carried via the nanoparticles, to the bad cells only. A second method will be to destroy cancer cells (identified by nanoparticles) using laser rays. Ultimately, technologies like this will allow doctors to deliver cancer treatment earlier, faster, and more **thoroughly**, with fewer side effects. Unfortunately, even though nanoparticles have great medical potential, there are serious concerns that these same materials could have negative environmental and health effects.

In recent studies, fish exposed to water containing large amounts of nanoparticles suffered brain damage. And people are at risk as well. After exposing lab-grown human cells to water containing large amounts of nanoparticles, researchers found that half the human cells died.

Because nanotechnology is so potentially useful, many scientists don't think research into its many uses should be stopped; learning more about nanotechnology should remain a **priority**. But scientists do believe that governments should **allocate** more money for safety-related studies—to make sure that large concentrations of nanoparticles do not get into our food and water supplies and cause serious problems.

Meanwhile, research into the uses of nanotechnology in health and many other fields continues. And it's evolving quickly. Even a decade ago, many of these applications "would have seemed pretty unrealistic," says chemist Vicki Colvin. Perhaps that old movie, *Fantastic Voyage,* isn't so hard to believe after all.

---

2 When a doctor **diagnoses** a disease, he or she identifies it.

3 A **dot** is a very small round mark, like a period (.).

4 When you have **nausea**, you feel like you're going to vomit.

Reading Comprehension

Multiple Choice. Choose the best answer for each question.

Gist
1. What is this reading mainly about?
   a. a fantastic voyage within the human body
   b. how nanotechnology can be used in medical science
   c. the dangers and side effects of nanotechnology
   d. the various ways of detecting cancer

Detail
2. How big is a nanometer?
   a. the size of a comma
   b. the same size as a quantum dot
   c. a billion nanoparticles wide
   d. one-billionth of a meter

Vocabulary
3. In line 44, the word *determine* could be replaced by _____.
   a. discover   b. report
   c. miss   d. hide

Detail
4. Exposing human cells to large amounts of nanoparticles _____.
   a. has no effect
   b. should remain a priority
   c. is how cancer can be treated
   d. can result in 50% cell death

Detail
5. Which of these statements about nanotechnology is NOT true?
   a. It could lead to early diagnosis of cancer.
   b. Doctors could potentially use it to destroy cancer cells.
   c. It will allow doctors to avoid destroying healthy cells.
   d. It is completely safe for humans and animals.

Main Idea
6. What is the main idea of the next-to-last paragraph
(starting line 84)?
   a. Nanotechnology has not proved useful, and most
      scientists want the research halted.
   b. Scientists want to see research into nanotechnology
      continue, but carefully.
   c. Nanotechnology is so useful that many governments
      are investing in research.
   d. Many scientists think that nanotechnology is too
      dangerous to be permitted.

Paraphrase
7. In the last paragraph, Vicki Colvin says that even a decade
ago, many of these applications "*would have seemed
pretty unrealistic.*" What does she mean?

   a. Nanotechnology has evolved a lot in the last decade.
   b. Ten years ago, nanotechnology applications weren't
      very realistic.
   c. Some of these applications are ten years old and so not
      very useful.
   d. In ten years, there have been few realistic applications
      for nanotechnology.

Critical Thinking

Inferring: Do you think the author is generally positive or negative about the future for nanotechnology? What makes you think so?

_____

Discussion: Do you think research into nanotechnology should continue? Why or why not?

Reading Skill

Understanding an Author's Use of Quotes

Authors sometimes enclose certain parts of a text within quotation marks (" "). An author may use quotes for various reasons, such as:

To indicate a definition:
The verb *transplant* means "to move an organ from one body to another."

To highlight a memorable phrase:
Dr. Christiaan Barnard was known as the "film star surgeon."

To show that a quote is a person's exact words:
He once said, "The prime goal is to alleviate suffering, not to prolong life."

To indicate a title of a short story or a chapter from a longer work.

A. Scan. Look back at the reading on pages 193–194. Find and underline the words and phrases that are in quotation marks below.

B. Inferring. Choose the most likely reason that the author used each quote.

1. "dwarf"
   a. to indicate a definition   b. to set off a title
   c. to highlight a memorable phrase   d. to express a person's exact words

2. "science of small"
   a. to indicate a definition   b. to set off a title
   c. to highlight a memorable phrase   d. to express a person's exact words

3. "would have seemed pretty unrealistic"
   a. to indicate a definition   b. to set off a title
   c. to highlight a memorable phrase   d. to express a person's exact words

∨ A ladybug on carbon nanotubes that are stretched between copper wires

Vocabulary Practice

A. Completion. Complete the information with the correct form of words from the box.

allocate	bond	inject	meanwhile
multiply	priority	radical	thorough

Cancer is one of the biggest killers in the world today, and finding ways to prevent and cure it is a medical **1.** _____. Every year, governments and private companies **2.** _____ huge amounts of money to cancer research. Here are two recent developments.

One development with a lot of potential is nanotechnology. Some scientists claim that it will be possible for doctors to **3.** _____ nanoparticles into a patient's body to find and attack cancer cells before these unhealthy cells **4.** _____ and **5.** _____ together to become a tumor.

6. _____, a(n) **7.** _____ new way to detect cancer uses dogs. It works on the fact that many animals' sense of smell is much better than that of a human. The method hasn't been **8.** _____ tested yet, but early studies have found that dogs can identify a person who has cancer by sniffing either sores on the skin or the person's breath.

∧ Skin cancer can be a particular problem for light-skinned people living in environments with a lot of sunlight. Australian beach lifeguard Don Bennewith has had over 600 skin cancers removed.

B. Matching. Match the words in the box with the definitions below. One word is extra.

allocate	extensive	insert	meanwhile	multiply	priority

1. something that is treated as the most important thing _____

2. to give to someone for use for a particular purpose _____

3. covering a wide range or area _____

4. to place or fit something into something else _____

5. during the time a particular thing is happening _____

Word Link The prefix **multi-** means "many," e.g., *multiply, multicolored, multimedia, multinational.*

VIRUS OUTBREAK: H5N1

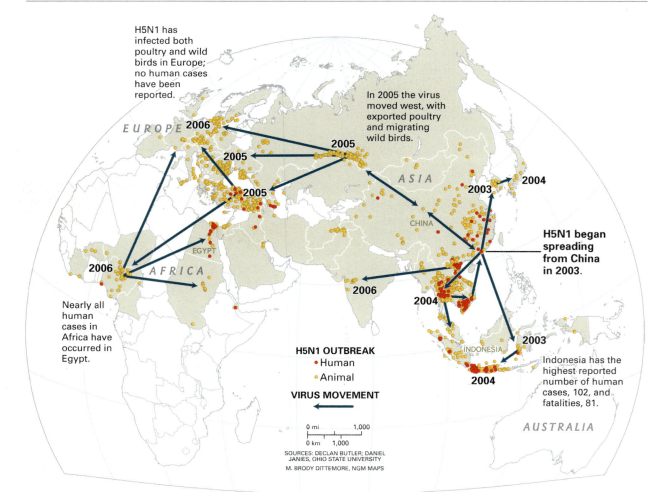

H5N1 has infected both poultry and wild birds in Europe; no human cases have been reported.

In 2005 the virus moved west, with exported poultry and migrating wild birds.

EUROPE **2006**

2005

2005

2005

ASIA

2005

2003 **2004**

CHINA

EGYPT

H5N1 began spreading from China in 2003.

2006 AFRICA

Nearly all human cases in Africa have occurred in Egypt.

2006

2004

H5N1 OUTBREAK
- Human
- Animal

VIRUS MOVEMENT

INDONESIA **2003**

2004

Indonesia has the highest reported number of human cases, 102, and fatalities, 81.

AUSTRALIA

0 mi 1,000
0 km 1,000

SOURCES: DECLAN BUTLER; DANIEL
JANIES, OHIO STATE UNIVERSITY
M. BRODY DITTEMORE, NGM MAPS

> ∧ A map showing the spread of the H5N1 virus, which is a kind of influenza sometimes known as "bird flu."

Before You Read

A. Discussion. Look at the map showing the spread of a virus. Then answer the questions.

1. When did the virus first occur?

2. On which continent was there the highest number of human cases?

3. Where were there cases of H5N1 in birds and not humans?

B. Predict. The passage on pages 199–201 is about zoonotic diseases. What do you think *zoonotic* means? Check (✓) your guess. Then read the passage to check your idea.

☐ diseases that spread very rapidly

☐ diseases that spread from animals to humans

☐ diseases that spread from humans to animals

☐ diseases that cannot be treated

DEADLY CONTACT

A veterinarian treats a horse following an outbreak of the Hendra virus in Australia.

1 Zoonotic diseases are on the rise around the globe. Researchers are in a race against time to be ready for the next big outbreak.

In September 1994, a violent disease erupted among a
5 group of racehorses in a small town in Australia. The first **victim** was a female horse that was last seen eating grass beneath a fruit tree. One of her caretakers noticed that the horse didn't appear to be well, and brought the animal back to her stable[1] for observation. Within hours, the horse's
10 health declined rapidly. Three people worked to save the animal—the horse's trainer, an assistant, and a veterinarian.[2] Nevertheless, the horse died two days later, leaving the cause of her death uncertain. Had she been bitten by a snake, or eaten something **poisonous**?

1 A **stable** is a building where horses or cattle are kept.
2 A **veterinarian** is a person who is qualified to treat diseased or injured animals.

Within two weeks, most of the other horses in the stable became ill as well. All had high **fevers**, difficulty breathing, facial **swelling**, and blood coming from their noses and mouths. Despite efforts by the veterinarian, 12 more animals died. Meanwhile, the trainer and his assistant also became ill, and within days, the trainer was dead, too. Laboratory analysis finally discovered the **root** of the problem: The horses and men had been infected by a previously unknown virus, which doctors eventually labeled Hendra. This virus had originated in bats that lived in the tree where the first horse had been eating grass. The virus passed from the bats to the horse, which then **transmitted** the virus to other horses and to people—with disastrous results.

The Virus Threat

Infectious disease is all around us. Disease-causing agents, such as viruses, usually have specific targets. Some viruses affect only humans. Other viruses live in or affect only animals. Problems start when animal viruses are able to infect people as well, a process known as zoonosis. When an animal virus passes to a human, the results can be fatal. Often, our immune systems are not **accustomed to** these viruses, and are unable to stop them before they harm us, and even kill us.

In the last three decades, more than 30 zoonotic diseases—the kind that live only in animals but somehow pass to people—have emerged around the globe. HIV is an example; it evolved from a virus originally carried by

∧ The Hendra outbreak was eventually traced to fruitbats, like this little red flying fox.

African monkeys and later, chimps. Today, **conservative** estimates suggest that HIV has infected more than 70 million people in the past three decades, though this number may be higher. SARS, a type of flu that jumped from chickens to humans, is another type of zoonotic disease.

But how do these viruses—like Hendra, SARS, and HIV—pass from animals to humans? Contact is crucial. Human destruction of animal habitats,[3] for example, is forcing wild animals to move closer to the places people live—putting humans at risk for exposure to animal viruses. The closer humans are to animals, the greater the risk of being bitten, scratched, or exposed to animal waste, which can enable a virus to pass from an animal to a human. Raising animals (for example, on a farm) or keeping certain kinds of wild animals (like monkeys) as pets increases the risk of exposure. Eating animals that are diseased can also result in a virus being transmitted.

Worldwide Travelers

The factor that is probably most responsible for the spread of zoonotic diseases worldwide is international travel. In 1999, for example, a deadly disease—one that had never been seen before in the Western Hemisphere—appeared in the United States. There were several **incidences** that year of both birds and people becoming sick and dying in New York City, and doctors couldn't explain why. Subsequently, they discovered that the deaths had been caused by the same thing: the West Nile virus, found typically in birds and transmitted by mosquitoes that live in parts of northern Africa. Somehow this virus—probably carried by an infected mosquito or bird on a plane or ship—arrived in the U.S. Now, birds and mosquitoes native to North America are carriers of this virus as well.

Scientist Eric Leroy studies the Ebola virus at his lab in Gabon. According to his research, fruit bats are carriers of the disease. ❯

West Nile cannot be transmitted from person to person. However, a zoonotic disease which can spread from human to human by a handshake or sneeze could create a major medical **emergency**: It could potentially circle the world and kill millions of people before science can find a way to control it.

Today, researchers are working to create vaccines[4] for many of these zoonotic diseases in the hope of controlling their impact on humans. Other specialists are trying to make communities more aware of disease prevention and treatment, and to help people understand that we are all—humans, animals, and insects—in this together.

---

3 An animal's or a plant's **habitat** is the natural environment where it normally lives and grows.

4 A **vaccine** is a harmless form of a disease given to people to prevent them from getting that disease.

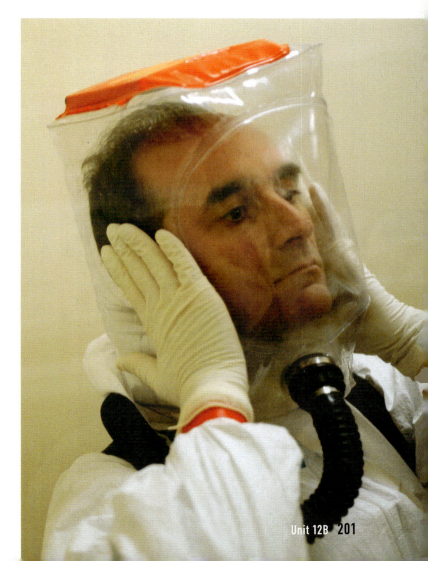

Reading Comprehension

Multiple Choice. Choose the best answer for each question.

Gist

1. What is this reading mainly about?
   a. the unexplained deaths of horses and humans
   b. the symptoms of zoonotic diseases seen in humans
   c. the effect of international travel on the spread of disease
   d. the rise in the spread of viruses from animals to humans

Cause and Effect

2. What caused the Australian racehorses to get sick?
   a. a virus spread by snakes
   b. a virus spread by bats
   c. a virus spread by humans
   d. a virus spread by a fruit tree

Vocabulary

3. The word *fatal* in line 40 could be replaced with _____.
   a. scary
   b. painful
   c. harmful
   d. deadly

Purpose

4. What is the purpose of paragraph 4 (from line 44)?
   a. to discuss the rise in zoonotic diseases in the past three decades
   b. to inform the reader where the HIV virus came from and how it evolved
   c. to give examples and explain the meaning of zoonotic diseases
   d. to compare the spread of HIV and SARS with other zoonotic diseases

Reference

5. In line 75, *a deadly disease* refers to _____.
   a. Hendra
   b. Ebola
   c. West Nile virus
   d. HIV

Detail

6. Which virus is NOT mentioned in the passage as being zoonotic?
   a. SARS
   b. HIV
   c. Flu
   d. Hendra

Detail

7. Which of these is NOT given as a reason for the increase in zoonotic diseases?
   a. raising animals
   b. destruction of habitat
   c. lower disease resistance
   d. international travel

Critical Thinking

Inferring: According to the article, in the last three decades, more than 30 zoonotic diseases have emerged worldwide. Apart from the reasons given, can you think of any other reason for this sharp increase?

_____

Discussion: What do you think people or governments should do to prevent zoonotic diseases from spreading to humans?

Inferring Information

Writers often tell readers more than they say directly. They give clues that help you "read between the lines" to get a deeper understanding of a text. Understanding these clues is called inferring, or drawing inferences. When you infer, you draw on background knowledge, common sense, and the details in the text. The following are examples of questions that ask you to infer information from a passage.

Which statement would the author most likely agree with?
Which statement is best supported by the passage?
According to the passage, we can reasonably infer that _____.
Based on the passage, it could be suggested that _____.

A. Inference. Look back at the last three paragraphs of the reading on page 201. Can you infer the following information? Circle **Yes** or **No**.

1. Some people have been infected by the West Nile virus from tourists in Egypt. **Yes** **No**

2. All zoonotic diseases can be spread by coughing. **Yes** **No**

3. Zoonotic diseases can spread extremely quickly. **Yes** **No**

4. It's possible to prevent zoonotic diseases. **Yes** **No**

5. Vaccines for most zoonotic diseases will be created within a few years. **Yes** **No**

B. Inference. Choose the best answer for each question.

1. Who is at the greatest risk of contracting a zoonotic disease?

   a. a nurse   b. a teacher   c. a chicken farmer

2. Which statement is best supported by the passage?

   a. Zoonotic diseases did not exist more than 30 years ago.

   b. Keeping but never touching a wild animal will keep you safe from zoonotic diseases.

   c. You won't get a virus from eating a diseased animal if you cook the meat well.

   d. People who regularly travel abroad are more likely to get a zoonotic disease.

Vocabulary Practice

A. Completion. Complete the information with the correct form of words from the box. One word is extra.

conservative	emergency	fever	incidence
root	swell	transmit	victim

Polio is a very serious disease, the **1.** _____ cause of which is a virus called *Poliovirus*. The virus is easily **2.** _____ to other humans through contact, especially in a humid or wet environment. It is particularly common in the summer. One of the first symptoms of polio is a high **3.** _____, making it seem like ordinary flu. Later, **4.** _____ of polio may suffer from varying degrees of paralysis[1] affecting the arms and legs. In severe cases, the heart and lung muscles are also paralyzed, causing death, unless **5.** _____ treatment is received.

In the first half of the 20th century, it was one of the most feared of childhood diseases, affecting, at a(n) **6.** _____ estimate, tens of thousands of people a year. There was great pressure to create a vaccine, and in the 1950s and '60s, vaccines created by Jonas Salk and Albert Sabin became widely available. This managed to reduce the global **7.** _____ of polio from many hundreds of thousands a year down to around a thousand.

_____

1 **Paralysis** is the loss of the ability to move and feel in all or part of your body.

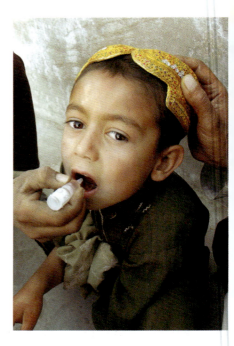

∧ A child receives the polio vaccine as part of an anti-polio vaccination program in Pakistan

B. Words in Context. Complete each sentence with the correct answer.

1. If something is **poisonous**, it is _____ to eat.

    a. safe   b. dangerous

2. When something **swells**, it becomes _____ in size.

    a. larger   b. smaller

3. You are more likely to be **accustomed to** something you have had _____.

    a. for a long time   b. for a short time

4. A **conservative** estimate of a number is probably _____ than the real number.

    a. higher   b. lower

> **Word Partnership**
> Use *emergency*
> with: (*adj.*) **major** emergency, **medical** emergency, **minor** emergency; (*n.*) **state of** emergency, emergency **care**, emergency **surgery**.